T0295807

Banking and Finance

This shortform book presents key peer-reviewed research selected by expert series editors and contextualised by new analysis from each author on how the specific field addressed has evolved.

The book features contributions on the development of banking regulation in Scotland, the role of commercial banking on the functioning of the British corporate economy, the impact of British monetary policy on small firm growth and the politics of corporate governance.

Of interest to business and economic historians, this shortform book also provides analysis that will be valuable reading across the social sciences.

John F. Wilson is Pro Vice-Chancellor (Business and Law) at Northumbria University at Newcastle. He has published widely in the fields of business, management and industrial history, including ten monographs, six edited collections and over seventy articles and chapters. Most notably, his *British Business History, 1720–1994* is still being used in UK universities. He was also the founding editor of the *Journal of Industrial History*, as well as co-editor of *Business History* for ten years.

Nicholas D. Wong is Vice-Chancellor's Senior Research Fellow at Newcastle Business School, Northumbria University. His research areas cover historical organisation studies and uses of the past, family business studies and entrepreneurship. He has published in *Business History, International Journal of Contemporary Hospitality Management* and *Entreprise et Histoire*. Nicholas won the John F. Mee Best Paper Award at the Academy of Management in 2018 for his contribution to the Management History Division.

Steven Toms spent fifteen years in senior management at Nottingham University as head of the undergraduate programme, chair of teaching committee and research director before becoming Head of York Management School in 2004. Professor Toms's research interests cover the role of accounting, accountability and corporate governance in the development of organisations, particularly from a historical perspective. He is interested in perspectives that integrate financial models with economic and organisational theory and corporate strategy. Specific applications range from business history – in particular cotton and other textiles trades – to capital markets and social and environmental accounting. He was Editor of the journal *Business History* from 2007 to 2013.

Routledge Focus on Industrial History
Series Editors: John F. Wilson, Nicholas D. Wong and Steven Toms

This shortform series presents key peer-reviewed research originally published in the *Journal of Industrial History*, selected by expert series editors and contextualised by new analysis from each author on how the specific field addressed has evolved.

Of interest to business historians, economic historians and social scientists interested in the development of key industries, the series makes theoretical and conceptual contributions to the field, as well as providing a plethora of empirical, illustrative and detailed case-studies of industrial developments in Britain, the United States and other international settings.

Published titles in this series include:

Growth and Decline of American Industry
Case Studies in the Industrial History of the USA
Edited by John F. Wilson, Nicholas D. Wong and Steven Toms

Management and Industry
Case Studies in UK Industrial History
Edited by John F. Wilson, Nicholas D. Wong and Steven Toms

Banking and Finance
Case Studies in the Development of the UK Financial Sector
Edited by John F. Wilson, Nicholas D. Wong and Steven Toms

Banking and Finance

Case Studies in the Development of the UK Financial Sector

Edited by John F. Wilson, Nicholas D. Wong and Steven Toms

LONDON AND NEW YORK

First published 2020
by Routledge
2 Park Square, Milton Park, Abingdon, Oxon OX14 4RN

and by Routledge
52 Vanderbilt Avenue, New York, NY 10017

Routledge is an imprint of the Taylor & Francis Group, an informa business

© 2020 selection and editorial matter, John F. Wilson, Nicholas D. Wong and Steven Toms; individual chapters, the contributors.

British Library Cataloguing-in-Publication Data
A catalogue record for this book is available from the British Library

Library of Congress Cataloging-in-Publication Data
A catalog record for this book has been requested

ISBN: 978-0-367-18006-5 (hbk)
ISBN: 978-0-429-05901-8 (ebk)

Typeset in Times New Roman
by Apex CoVantage, LLC

Contents

List of contributors   viii

Introduction   1
JOHN F. WILSON, NICHOLAS D. WONG AND STEVEN TOMS

1 **The move to limited liability banking in Scotland
   and the introduction of bank regulation**   6
   JOHN D. TURNER

2 **The commercial banking industry and its part in the
   emergence and consolidation of the corporate economy
   in Britain before 1940**   30
   PETER WARDLEY

3 **Did they have it so good? Small firms and British
   monetary policy in the 1950s**   69
   FRANCESCA CARNEVALI

4 **Corporate governance in a political climate: the 'City',
   the government and British Leyland Motor
   Corporation**   95
   SUE BOWDEN

Index   130

Contributors

Sue Bowden is Director of the Centre for Historical Economics and Related Studies at The University of York.

Francesca Carnevali (1964–2013) was awarded her PhD by the London School of Economics. She spent most of her career at Birmingham University (UK), first in the economic history department then later in the history department. She has been Visiting Scholar at Harvard University and the London School of Economics. Francesca was a very active scholar in both economic and business history, publishing articles in the major journals of both disciplines, as well as monographs and edited books, on a wide variety of topics. These include the role of institutions, the functioning of industrial districts, the impact of finance and banking on manufacturing and the economy, and the issue of luxury.

John D. Turner is Professor of Finance and Financial History at Queen's University Belfast. He is the former Head of Queen's Management School, serving in that capacity from 2014 until 2017. He is also the founder and director of the Queen's University Centre for Economic History. He has recently published an award-winning book with Cambridge University Press titled *Banking in Crisis: The Rise and Fall of British Banking Stability*. His next book, which will be published by Cambridge University Press in 2020, is titled *Boom and Bust: A Global History of Financial Bubbles*. He has held several distinguished visiting positions during his career – he has been a Houblon-Norman Fellow at the Bank of England and an Alfred D. Chandler Fellow at Harvard Business School. He is currently the editor of the *Economic History Review*.

Peter Wardley, a former lecturer in economic history at the universities of Swansea, Hull, Aberdeen, Leicester, Nottingham and Durham, joined

Bristol Polytechnic to be thereafter employed for twenty-eight years at UWE, Bristol. He has published numerous articles and chapters on topics that largely relate, in one way or another, to the collection, presentation, distribution and analysis of information, either by contemporaries or, subsequently, by historians. In the latter context, he was Information Technology Review Editor of the *Economic History Review* and edited the *Bristol Historical Resource CD*. Meanwhile his historical research has investigated: the diffusion of Hindu-Arabic numerals in early seventeenth century Britain; the development of inter-company information transfers within trade associations; and, the co-introduction of women and mechanisation in interwar Britain banking. The Nuffield Foundation generously supported his investigation of this well-managed corporate innovation that is reported in this collection. He has also published articles on two inter-related topics: the growth of 'Big Business' in the twentieth century world economy and the emerging pre-eminence and significance of the service sector for modern economic growth. More recently, he has been Visiting Professor at the Universitat Pompeu Fabra, Barcelona.

Introduction

*John F. Wilson, Nicholas D. Wong
and Steven Toms*

Purpose and significance of the series

The concept of the *Routledge Series of Industrial History* was motivated by the desire of the editors to provide an outlet for articles
originally published in the defunct *Journal of Industrial History* (*JIH*).
By utilising this extensive repository of top-quality publications, the
series will ensure that the authors' findings will contribute to recent
debates in the field of management and industrial history. Indeed,
the articles contained in these volumes will appeal to a wide audience, including business historians, economic historians and social
scientists interested in longitudinal studies of the development of key
issues, industries and themes. Moreover, the series will provide fresh
insight into how the academic field has developed in the last twenty
years, frequently offering a Postscript by the author(s) that will assess
how the specific field addressed has changed over the course of the
last twenty years.

The editors believe that the quality of scholarship evident in the
articles originally published in the *JIH* now deserves a much broader
audience. The peer-reviewed articles are built on robust business-
historical research methodologies and are subject to extensive primary
research. The series will make important theoretical and conceptual
contributions to the field, as well as providing a plethora of empirical,
illustrative and detailed case-studies of industrial developments in
Britain, the United States and other international settings. The collection will be of interest to a broad spectrum of social scientists,
and especially business school and history department academics, as
they provide valuable material that can be used in both teaching and
research.

Building on the original *Journal of Industrial History*

The first edition of the *Journal of Industrial History* was published in 1998, with the aim of providing 'clear definitional parameters for industrial historians' and, in turn establishing links between 'industrial history and theoretical work in social science disciplines like economics, management (including international business), political science, sociology, and anthropology'. As it is over twenty years since its original publication, it is clear that the relevance of the *JIH* has stood the test of time. The original *JIH* volumes covered a diverse range of topics, including: industrial structure and behaviour, especially in manufacturing and services; industrial and business case-studies; business strategy and structure; nationalisation and privatisation; globalisation and competitive advantage; business culture and industrial development; education, training and human resources; industrial relations and its institutions; the relationship between financial institutions and industry; industrial politics, including the formulation and impact of industrial and commercial policy; and industry and technology. The current *Routledge Series of Industrial History* will provide a cross-section of articles that cover the themes and topics, many of which remain central to management studies. These include separate volumes covering 'management and industry'; 'industry in the USA'; and 'banking and finance'. Future volumes in the series will cover 'case-studies in British industrial history'; 'technology'; and 'cotton and textile industry'. The *Routledge Series of Industrial History* will reframe highly original material that illustrates a wide variety of themes in management and organisation studies, including entrepreneurship, strategy, family business, trust, networks and international business, focusing on topics such as growth of the firm, crisis management, governance, management and leadership.

Volume Three: contribution and key findings

The third volume of this series is focused on the theme of 'banking and finance', including articles that examine the development of a broad range of topics related to different forms of banking, British monetary policy and governance covering the period from the late nineteenth century until the late twentieth century. This volume will survey the debates related to a diverse range of financial institutions and the impact that macroeconomic policy and political regulations can have in the functions and liquidity of banks, large and smaller firms.

The first chapter, 'The move to limited liability banking in Scotland and the introduction of bank regulation', is a study by John Turner that provides historical insights into the development of limited liability banking in Scotland and the subsequent move towards greater regulation of the banking industry during the nineteenth and twentieth centuries. The chapter highlights how, prior to 1882, the Scottish banking system had operated in a system of unlimited liability and as a result being virtually free of government regulations. After 1882, the Scottish banking system moved towards a system of limited liability, which was subsequently underwritten by the Bank of England. The emphasis of the study covers the implications of the move from unlimited to limited liability and the impact this had on the development of regulation and increased supervision by the Bank of England. In addition to providing keen insights into the functions and operating of the banking system, the chapter also provides new perspectives on the role of state interference and government regulation on the ability of private banks to manage risk. The chapter concludes by highlighting how increasing deregulation of the banking systems worldwide can lead to greater banking instability; a prediction that was proved accurate by the 2008 financial crisis.

The second chapter, 'The commercial banking industry and its part in the emergence and consolidation of the corporate economy in Britain before 1940' by Peter Wardley, focuses on the role of commercial banking on the functioning of the British corporate economy. This chapter is neatly structured around the development of three overarching themes: firstly, Wardley establishes the importance of banking as a service institution in the modern British economy; secondly, the study links the performance of the financial sector to other sectors in the British economy; and finally, the chapter furthers the debates around the consolidation of banks as large corporations and the subsequent development of organisational structures designed to enhance the performance of banks in shifting economic and commercial contexts. Building on Chandler's work, Wardley produces a picture of the development of British commercial banking with reference to the role of entrepreneurship and management in the process of growth of the corporate economy. The chapter provides fresh insights into the development of hierarchical bureaucratic systems in Britain that not only divorced ownership from control, but also facilitated the growth of strategic, operational and functional capabilities. This, in turn, shaped British corporate culture in Britain during the latter part of the twentieth century.

The third chapter by Francesca Carnevali, 'Did they have it so good? Small firms and British monetary policy in the 1950s', examines the impact of British monetary policy on the ability of small firms to advance growth. The chapter illustrates how government policy and restrictions on bank lending affected small firms more harshly than larger organisations because they had no other source of funding beyond the banks. The chapter provides insight into the 'Macmillan Gap' which saw overdraft provisions for small firms curtailed and resulted in credit restriction, forcing business owners to undertake costly credit or hire purchase initiatives in order to expand, diversify or purchase new machinery. In particular, the chapter provides new perspectives on the utility of hire purchase for industrial purposes. The study concludes by highlighting how small firms were forced by British monetary policy and subsequent credit restriction to use overdraft facilities to facilitate expansion, resulting in the widening of the 'Macmillan Gap'. This forced small firms to source external funding creatively in an attempt to facilitate the transition from small- to medium-sized enterprise.

The final chapter in the volume, 'Corporate governance in political climate: the 'City', government and British Leyland Motor Company' by Sue Bowden, addresses a gap in the literature by using corporate governance as a lens to understand the mechanisms whereby a record of under-performance might or might not be reversed. By combining context with data, Bowden is able to analyse corporate governance and share transactions and uncover how this is impacted by the political climate. Ultimately, the chapter provides insight into three crucial areas: firstly, it examines how ownership and managerial responsibilities in British Leyland Motor Company (BLMC) were exercised; this is followed by an assessment of the role public policy played in determining organisational behaviour; and finally, Bowden assesses how and why a record of underperformance may not be corrected. Using a novel approach that combines principal-agent and game theory, the chapter is able to shed light on the actions of key protagonists at BLMC and how this influenced the strategy of the firm. Moreover, the case-study illustrates the tension between small and large shareholders and the concepts of 'lock-in' and 'short-termism' that in an uncertain political climate can result in the irreversible decline of large companies.

Conclusion

It is apparent from this brief review of the chapters that the third volume in the series makes important contributions to the field of industrial history in several ways. Firstly, it provides a series of high calibre and unique studies in aspects of British economic development during the nineteenth and twentieth century, foreshadowing more recent debates on banking structures, governance and the effect of macroeconomic policy and regulation on the performance of both large and small firms. Secondly, the chapters shed light on the broader subjects of government and public policy, industrial performance in times of crisis and uncertainty, the influence of shareholders in governing strategy and the evolution of the British corporate economy. Finally, the volume provides strong historical case-studies that can be used by students and researchers who are exploring issues related to the evolution and development of British financial institutions and the role they played in the development of organisational culture, the strategy and performance of companies in different industries and of contrasting scale and scope. The editors believe that this volume will not only provide a much wider audience for articles that link into a range of topical issues but also feed into debates in the wider social sciences. These are themes that will be developed further in subsequent volumes of the *Routledge Series of Industrial History*, highlighting the intrinsic value in republishing material from the *Journal of Industrial History* and ensuring that the articles contribute extensively to current debates.

Chapter 1

The move to limited liability banking in Scotland and the introduction of bank regulation*

John D. Turner

I

Over the last two decades there has been a huge interest in the Scottish banking system of the nineteenth century.[1] This interest has been sparked by the modern free banking school of economists who argue that banks do not need to be regulated by government, and that the 'fragility and instability of real-world banking systems is not a free-market phenomenon, but a consequence of legal restrictions'.[2] The modern free bankers argue that the Scottish banking system up until 1845 was relatively free from government regulation, this explaining the stability of the system. It is argued here that the Scottish banking system was stable up until 1882 because the private banks were required to have unlimited liability. The unlimited liability of equity holders gave the noteholders and depositors of Scottish banks a credible commitment of ex post contractual performance. Essentially, the period before 1882 can be viewed as one free from government regulation of banks. In 1882, the private banks moved to a limited liability status, and from then, the stability of the Scottish banking system was underwritten by the Bank of England.

Section two examines the reasons why unlimited liability prevented banks engaging in opportunism, and it also discusses the stability of the Scottish banking system under unlimited liability. In section three, the move to limited liability is discussed, and it is argued that the introduction of the lender of last resort was the institutional change which enabled the Scottish banks to move to a limited liability status. Section four investigates the stability of the Scottish banking system before and after the move to limited liability. Section five examines the subsequent development of regulation and supervision by the Bank of England and the final section is a brief conclusion which discusses some policy implications.

II

To what extent can the equity holders of a limited liability bank engage in ex post opportunistic behaviour at a noteholder's or depositor's expense? This, in accordance with the analyses of Williamson[3] and Alchian and Woodward,[4] will depend on the plasticity of a bank's assets. The main asset of any bank is its loan portfolio which is difficult to value at any point in time due to the absence of a market price; and the information necessary to value the portfolio of loans will not be available because borrowers place a high value on a bank's loan discreteness. This implies that depositors cannot monitor the loan portfolio of the bank. Hence, banks' loan portfolios are highly plastic due to the information asymmetry which exists because of a bank's discreteness about its loans. Therefore, sufficiently motivated boards of directors acting on behalf of equity holders can engage in a large degree of ex post opportunistic behaviour.

Banks are typically very highly leveraged firms compared to most non-bank firms. This implies that equity holders have the ability to engage in ex post opportunistic behaviour to an even greater extent. The banking firm differs from other types of firms in another important way. The value of a debt claim held by depositors/noteholders depends not on its intrinsic value, but rather on the value of the assets of the bank, particularly the loan portfolio. Due to the plasticity of these assets, the cost of information to determine their value is prohibitive. For a bank, the marginal cost of printing or issuing a debt claim against itself is essentially zero, while the value of the debt claim, if redeemed, is its money value. A bank therefore has an incentive to lower its asset value in each time period (by taking on riskier projects and issuing as money as many claims as possible). This implies that a bank enjoys a quasi-rent each period, the value of which is dependent upon the ability of the bank to lower its asset value.

In the absence of a credible commitment of ex post contractual performance, a non-existence problem may occur in that risk-averse depositors/noteholders will refuse to hold the bank's claims at any risk premium. As Bagehot eloquently put it: 'till it [a bank] is trusted it is nothing, and when it ceases to be trusted it returns to nothing'.[5] Therefore, it is in the interests of bank equity holders and depositors that some credible commitment to ex post contractual performance exists.[6]

The equity holders of the unlimited liability Scottish banks assured noteholders and depositors of ex post contractual performance because if they engaged in opportunism and defaulted, they had to cover any shortfall between public liabilities and assets plus capital out of their own personal wealth. The unlimited liability of the Scottish banks gave noteholders and depositors a credible commitment that the banks would not engage in opportunism.

However, the three public banks had a limited liability status. Why then did noteholders and depositors trust the public banks? The public banks were set up by Parliament, and they dealt with public business such as remittance of revenue from customs and excise, and payment of armed forces.[7] A. W. Kerr viewed the public banks as semi-government functionaries.[8] In a similar vein, Checkland argues that the State had not only created the public banks but had 'continued to confirm their preferred position, through their limited liability and through their public identity and perpetual succession'.[9] Checkland further adds weight to the concept that the public banks were essentially State banks by stating that: 'the selection and manipulation of the boards of directors of the public banks was part of the general political control of Scotland, just as was the manning of Edinburgh town council'.[10] This suggests that these banks, as public banks, had the full backing of the State and were run in the interests of the country. This in turn would have demonstrated a credible commitment to the banking public that the public banks would not engage in opportunism.

Furthermore, the charters of the public banks controlled the amount of capital these banks could issue; it forbade them from engaging in any other business apart from banking; and in some charters, it limited the amount of liabilities that a public bank could issue.[11] These requirements would have prevented the public banks engaging in opportunism, and would suggest a reason why Campbell[12] found that the limited liability public banks were more risk-averse than the private unlimited liability banks. Table I suggests that the public banks were required to keep a high percentage of their notes and deposits covered by shareholder capital, and this again demonstrates the prudent behaviour of the public banks. The most likely reason the public banks acted in a prudent manner was because their behaviour was constrained by the State. Furthermore, the public banks could be viewed as unlimited liability banks because they had the implicit back-up of taxpayers' money, and their behaviour was constrained by the State so that they conducted their business as if they had unlimited liability.

The unlimited liability of the private banks meant that noteholders and depositors were interested in the appropriable wealth of each individual equity holder. To ensure that equity holders had adequate wealth to cover any call made upon them in the event of bankruptcy, depositors could have monitored the observable assets of the main shareholders of the

Table 1.1 The public banks versus other banks

	Public Banks (£1000's)				Non-public Scottish Banks (£1000's)			
	Capital (c)	Notes (n)	Deposits (d)	c/(n+d)	Capital (c)	Notes (n)	Deposits (d)	c/(n+d)
1744	125	55	74	0.97	25	0	50	0.50
1772	184	139	331	0.39	212	505	518	0.21
1802	2520	1658	2406	0.62	765	1290	3386	0.16
1825	3864	1075	5809	0.56	2196	2187	8758	0.20

Source: Checkland, *Scottish Banking A History*, pp. 84, 237, 240, 424 and 426.

Notes: The figures for 1772 exclude the infamous Ayr Bank.

bank. In Scotland a Register of Sasines existed in which all land transactions were recorded.[13]

This register was open to public inspection, so it was very easy for the public to view how much property a bank equity holder possessed. However, this would only have indicated to depositors how much landed wealth an equity holder possessed. The commercial assets of some equity holders could also be costlessly ascertained by depositors. Depositors would not need to monitor every equity holder, only the most prominent ones who could be monitored at least cost. Depositors could then reasonably assume that it would be in the prominent equity holders' interest to ensure that all other equity holders had adequate wealth. For example, the directors of the Clydesdale bank had to meet two requirements: a) they had to be shareholders; and b) their main place of business had to be in the city of Glasgow or its neighbourhood.[14] These requirements would have meant that depositors/noteholders could have easily observed the appropriable wealth of the directors.

However, in the last period, equity holders, realising that their bank was about to become bankrupt, could sell their shares to someone with inadequate wealth to pay the extended liability. If unlimited liability is to be enforceable, transferability of shares must in some way be impaired in order to prevent shares being sold to partners with inadequate appropriable wealth.[15]

Prior to 1825, there was only one joint-stock bank established in Scotland, namely the Commercial Bank in 1810. The provincial banking companies were essentially large co-partneries and:

'shares in co-partneries were nominally freely transferable but in practice there were limitations on this. The Dundee Banking Co. in 1826 granted the right to shareholders "to sell and transfer the whole, or any of their shares, to any person or persons they please; provided such person or persons shall be approved of by the directors"'.[16]

Therefore, in order to assure depositors that shareholders would not sell their shares at the first sign of trouble, the shares in the Scottish co-partneries were not freely transferable. The directors of the company, being shareholders themselves, would have an incentive to set minimum wealth requirements for potential shareholders. Furthermore, partners were usually prohibited from holding shares in other banks.[17] This requirement would have given further assurance to depositors that shareholders had adequate wealth to cover any potential losses.

Starting with the Commercial in 1810, unlimited liability joint-stock banks were established in Scotland. By 1845, there were only three provincial banking companies remaining and most banking services were provided by twelve joint-stock banks and the three public banks. Once shares in an extended liability firm are freely transferable, the firm is essentially a de facto limited liability firm.[18] Were the joint-stock banks de facto limited liability banks? An article in the *Economist* in 1879 (a publication that was in favour of limited liability banking) suggests that the joint-stock banks were de facto limited liability banks, this being illustrated in the following quotation: 'the limited liability of the wealthy may be expected to prove as good if not a better security to the depositor as the unlimited liability of the poor'.[19] Were the shares of the Scottish banks in the possession of the poor? There are several things which suggest that this was not the case.

Firstly, the Scottish joint-stock banks published the names of their equity holders on an annual basis and these names would have been held in the Public Records Office. This would have aided depositors in monitoring the most prominent equity holders.

Secondly, as with the provincial banks, shares in the joint-stock banks were not freely transferable. Shares could only be transferred with the consent of the Board of Directors.[20] Indeed, for the Clydesdale Bank, much of the time at the weekly Board meeting was taken up in authorising share transfers.[21] It may have been the case that equity holders retained liability for a certain period after selling their share.[22] This would mean that when a share was sold the seller had an incentive to find out whether or not the buyer of the share had adequate wealth to cover the extended liability.

Thirdly, joint-stock bank failures did not result in any loss to depositors. In 1857, the Western Bank was the premier bank of Glasgow and the second bank in Scotland.[23] On the 9 November 1857, the Western

Bank failed, but 'the public lost nothing, for unlimited liability was still the rule'.[24]

The City of Glasgow Bank failure in 1878 also did not result in any losses for noteholders and depositors. However, after the liquidation, only 254 of the 1819 shareholders were solvent. For every £100 share held, a call was made for £2,750.[25] Does the fact that most shareholders became bankrupt imply that individuals with inadequate wealth held shares? The average weekly earnings in 1878 for a manual worker were approximately £1.24.[26] This suggests that the £2,750 paid by each shareholder in 1878 was a considerable amount of money, and that shares in the Glasgow City were not necessarily in the hands of those unable to pay the calls made upon them within the range that might reasonably have been expected.

Finally, in 1878, the average share price of the unlimited liability joint-stock banks was £185.09.[27] Even if share prices were issued at a low price, shareholders may have been required to hold more than one share. Clydesdale shares were issued at £20 each, but each shareholder had to hold a minimum of ten shares.[28] This is further evidence to suggest that shares in joint-stock banks were not owned by the poor.

How stable was the Scottish banking system under unlimited liability? This could be measured either by counting the number of bank failures or by examining the losses to depositors and noteholders.[29] Table 1.2 lists the failures of all Scottish provincial banks and joint-stock banks. Only five of these failures actually provided a loss for the public (and it is interesting to note that all the banks which produced

Table 1.2 Failures of Scottish provincial banks and joint-stock banks

Name of Bank	Failed	Number of partners	Loss to public
Douglas Heron & Co.	1772	241	None
Glasgow Arms Bank	1793	4	None
Merchant's Bank	1798	48	None
Merchant's Bank Stirling	1808	7	14/9 per £1
Dumfries Commercial Bank	1808	3	10/- per £1
Falkirk Union Banking Company	1816	6	9/6 per £1
East Lothian Banking Company	1822	58	None
Stirling Banking Company	1825	7	None
John Maberly & Co., Aberdeen	1833	1	£116,000 in total
Renfrewshire Banking Company	1842	3	9/3 per £1
Western Bank of Scotland	1857	1280	None
City of Glasgow Bank	1878	1819	None

Sources: Checkland, *Scottish Banking A History;* Munn, *The Scottish Provincial Banking Companies*

losses for the public had less than seven partners). This finding suggests that unlimited liability banks need a threshold of shareholders to
make them viable. It is for this reason that Thomas Joplin campaigned
for an end to the six-partner rule in England.[30] However, the dilution of
ownership means that the likelihood of a bank engaging in opportunism
increases as the number of partners grows. There is an alternative explanation for the phenomenon highlighted in Table 1.2. The more partners
a bank has, the larger it will be and the better able to diversify its risk.
Unlimited liability banking does not mean that there will be no bank
failures; however, it should prevent a systemic crisis and depositors suf-
fering financial losses.

So far in this section it has been argued that the stability of the Scottish banking system prior to 1882 was built on the bedrock of unlimited
liability. However, it is claimed that there are several other features of the
Scottish banking system which secured its stability. Firstly, it is claimed
that the note exchange helped create a stable banking system by prevent-
ing banks from aggressively overissuing.[31]

However, if enough banks overissue in an aggressive fashion, then
non-aggressive banks facing such a situation will be driven, in self-
defence, to take up the system of overtrading adopted by their competitors.[32] Furthermore, and importantly, a note exchange will not prevent
banks from overissuing deposits.

Secondly, it is claimed that the Bank of Scotland and Royal Bank of
Scotland acted as the policemen of the system.[33] This role performed
by the two public banks may have added to the stability of the Scottish
banking system. However, regulation/supervision cannot be undertaken
effectively by a commercial competitor because of conflicts of interest.[34]
Furthermore, the role of the public banks as 'leaders of the system' was
greatly weakened by the time of the 1830s due to the development of the
new joint-stock banks.[35]

III

It was only in 1855 that British Company Law granted freedom of incor-
poration. In 1855, the Limited Liability Act permitted British firms, apart
from banks and insurance companies, to become limited companies. The
Companies Act of 1862 permitted banks and insurance companies to
become limited liability companies.[36]

After the 1862 Companies Act, very few banks actually became limited companies apart from a few overseas and small banks e.g. Overend

Gurney.[37] Why did so few banks move to a limited liability status after the 1862 Act? White[38] argues that the fact banks chose to retain unlimited liability in Scotland for a further twenty years suggests that unlimited liability was an optimal arrangement. He argues that the Scottish banks eventually became limited in 1882, due to a change in shareholder's risk perceptions caused by the failure of the City of Glasgow Bank in 1878.

Evans and Quigley[39] argue that for banks to move to a limited liability status requires credible information and credible commitments. They suggest that the publication of independently audited balance sheets was the main innovation that provided depositors with the information necessary to facilitate Scottish banks moving from unlimited to limited liability banking. A contemporary commentator argued in a similar vein, that no unlimited liability bank should be permitted to become limited unless it published its accounts, and submitted to an independent audit.[40]

This view is flawed because provision of balance sheets does not solve the asymmetric information problem which exists between bank shareholders and depositors. A balance sheet reveals very little about the quality of the bank's asset portfolio since it principally consists of loans to borrowers. Borrowers from a bank place a high value upon a bank's discreteness about its loans and, as argued previously, this creates an asymmetry of information between the shareholders of the bank and its depositors. Furthermore, the independent nature of audits is highly questionable, casting doubt upon the veracity of the audit.[41]

In 1862, 'both in Scotland and England, it was supposed that for a prominent concern to register as a limited company would be a suggestion of weakness that might impair its credit'.[42] Similarly, Wilson states that unlimited liability was 'thought by the shareholders more conducive to profit, and by the depositors, more likely to give safety'.[43] Banks can only be trusted whenever depositors are given a credible commitment of ex post contractual performance. When bank shareholders have unlimited liability, depositors are assured of ex post contractual performance. If liability is limited, then depositors will not trust banks unless their behaviour is constrained or restrained by government. In 1862, there was no indication of banks being constrained or restrained by government, and furthermore, the Bank of England's lender of last resort (LOLR) function was not fully established at this stage. By 1875, twenty-four new limited banks had been established in the UK and many of these banks had previously been small private banks.[44] The failure of Overend Gurney in 1866 (Overend Gurney had just moved to a limited status in the previous year) gravely imperilled the position of the new limited liability banks. It is not surprising then that 'the experiences of the crisis stiffened the reluctance of many of the larger, old-established joint stock banks to accept a form of limited liability'.[45]

From 1862, and even before, the majority of economic commentators argued that banks should move towards a limited liability status. However, it took the failure of the City of Glasgow Bank in 1878, as well as the development of the last resort lending function by the Bank of England, before banks could move to a limited liability status. It is argued here that banks were unable to move to a limited liability status in 1862 because depositors of a bank would not have had a credible commitment of ex post contractual performance. The reason that banks in England and Wales were able to move in 1879 to a limited liability status was because the Bank of England had accepted its role as LOLR, and banks were able to apply to the Bank for last resort assistance.

Most banks in England moved to limited liability status after the 1879 Companies Act,[46] but it was 1882 before the seven unlimited Scottish banks changed their status to limited liability. An article in *The Banker's Magazine* states, with an element of surprise, that:

> 'One would have thought that, having had such bitter experience of the dangers and the hardships of unlimited liability, the Scotch banks would have been amongst the first to abandon a system which had proved so fruitful of disaster; and the energy with which they combated some, to them obnoxious, clauses it was sought to introduce into the Act, encouraged the belief that they were anxious to come under it'.[47]

Why did it take until April 1882 for the Scottish banks to move to a limited liability status? After the 1879 Company Act, Scottish banks were harangued in the press for not becoming limited. The reason they didn't, according to Kerr,[48] was that the banks were worried about the effect the name 'ABC Bank Ltd' might have on depositors. The unlimited liability banks may have been particularly worried about this because the three public banks refused to put the term 'limited' after their names.[49] This objection by the three public banks is said to have prevented the other seven unlimited banks from moving to a limited liability status.[50] This explanation suggests that depositors are irrational in that they did not know that the three public banks were limited because they did not have the term 'limited' after their names.

It is argued here that the Scottish banks did not move to limited liability status because the banks and depositors were unsure whether or not the Bank of England would act as a LOLR in Scotland. The provision of government insurance under limited liability shifts the risk of bank failure away from depositors, therefore depositors are willing to enter into contractual arrangements with banks. To assure the Scottish banks that they had access to the Bank of England discount window for last resort lending, it was granted to the Scottish banks in their charters in 1882.[51] The Scottish banks had been permitted to establish branches in London prior to the adoption of limited liability.[52] This would have meant that the Scottish banks had easy physical access to the discount window when the Bank of England began to act as a LOLR to the Scottish banking system.

Among economic historians,[53] it is accepted that by the late 1870s, the public believed that the Bank of England would act as lender of last resort to the banking system and, 'the Bank did nothing to disturb that belief'.[54] Prior to the late 1870s, the Bank of England did not bail out insolvent banks, but it did offer assistance to banks facing liquidity problems. However, after the move to limited liability, the Bank of England did bail out insolvent banks such as Barings, Yorkshire Penny Bank, William Deacon's Bank and Anglo-South American Bank (ASAB).[55] In all these bailouts, the Bank of England cajoled the main commercial banks into providing funds for the bailout.

IV

Once the Bank of England began to underwrite the liabilities of Scottish banks, depositors would have been no longer interested in whether or not their banks were engaging in opportunism since liability had been shifted onto the Bank of England. It is not surprising that Hankey said that the Bank's adoption of the LOLR role was 'the most mischievous doctrine ever broached in the monetary or banking world'.[56]

Did any contractual mechanisms exist to limit this moral hazard problem? The Companies Act 1879 required banks to have reserve liability by extending equity holders' liability to a fixed proportion of paid-up capital. The rationale for limited liability is that it permits equity holders to buy and sell shares to accommodate changes in their consumption, and this implies that a limited liability firm will have to have anonymous equity holders and free transferability of shares.[57] Under conditions of equity holder anonymity and free transferability, shares in reserve liability banks will be very quickly transferred to those with insufficient funds to provide multiple backing. Therefore, reserve liability will be of little use in restraining banks from engaging in opportunism.[58] The Free

Banking laws in ante-bellum US required free banks to have double liability; however, as the free banking crises demonstrated, double liability did not restrain the free banks from engaging in opportunism.[59]

Goodhart argues that up until the 1960s, the UK banking system was self-regulated by cartelised banking clubs, and this avoided the moral hazard problem.[60] In Scotland, the Committee of General Managers essentially operated a cartel which prohibited price competition.[61] However, non-price competition was permitted, and banks could circumvent the cartel by making loans through its London office.[62] A cartel prohibiting price competition does not prevent a banking system becoming more risky as banks can move in tandem to riskier positions. In the last quarter of the nineteenth century, Australian banks operated a similar price-setting cartel.[63] However, this cartel did not prevent the disastrous banking crisis of 1893. It is suggested here that after the move to limited liability, the Scottish banks were not restrained from engaging in opportunism, and the main thing that eventually reduced this problem was the Bank of England's use of moral suasion.

Bagehot's views on banking were that a limited liability system was more stable than an unlimited liability system, and that the presence of a LOLR made banking even more stable.[64] He believed that the moral hazard problem could be dealt with by providing last resort lending infrequently and at a punitive rate. His views were widely accepted, and it comes as little surprise that there was very little monitoring of commercial banks until after the Barings crisis in 1890. In the absence of monitoring and contractual restraints upon banks, it is predicted that the move to limited liability banking would result in banks being able to increase their risk-taking, which in turn leads to an increase in banking instability.

Banking instability is typically measured by counting the number of bank failures.[65] However, in a regime where the central bank commits to bail out banks, one would expect to witness no or very few failures, but this does not mean that the banking system is stable. Therefore, in this paper, banking instability is determined by examining the variance and skewness of the distribution of the annual returns on equity for each bank which existed both prior to and after the move to limited liability.[66] Historically, once banks have been insured, governments have imposed regulatory regimes which have encouraged banks to have similar risk-return profiles.[67] Essentially, when banks are insured, governments want what is known as a pooling equilibrium.[68] A large variance suggests that some banks have different risk-return profiles than other banks and that a pooling equilibrium is not being achieved. This suggests that some banks are engaging in opportunism. Furthermore, the skewness will show the propensity of banks to move to riskier positions.

It could be argued that these 'measures' of instability might be simply picking up changes in the economic environment. If the mean rate of return on equity was being used, this criticism would be valid. For example, there is a steady rise in the mean rate of return from 1896 to 1920. This could be merely reflecting the increase in world prices. From 1920 to 1940, there is a steady decline in the mean rate of return. This could be explained by the re-stocking boom of 1919–1920 and the subsequent collapse of asset values. This meant that banks were left with non-performing loans which had to be carried through the 1920s and then unravelled in the 1930s.[69] However, the variance and skewness of rates of return on equity should be low no matter what the economic conditions are like because a pooling equilibrium with banks having similar risk-return profiles is wanted.

The City of Glasgow Bank is excluded from the measure because we want to see whether the move to limited liability changed the behaviour of banks which existed prior to 1882. The public banks are included in the measure because, as previously argued, they essentially were unlimited liability banks since they had the implicit back-up of taxpayers' money. This measure of instability has one severe limitation – a health-warning needs to be attached to most profit figures since a certain amount of window-dressing will probably take place.[70] The implicit assumption being made here is that banks window-dressed their profits to similar degrees.

The data for Figures 1.1 and 1.2 were obtained from the Scottish Banking Collection at the University of Glasgow and from various issues of *The Bankers' Magazine*. Figure 1.1 shows variance measured using a three-year moving average. It is worth noting that the failure of the City of Glasgow Bank had little impact upon the stability of the other banks. After the move to limited liability, there is a slight increase in instability, but from the early 1890s, there is a rapid increase in the measure of instability. The explanation for this is found in the bailout of Barings in 1890 which signalled to banks that they could engage in riskier behaviour. The bailout was 'a dangerous precedent, the justification for which would be applicable to numerous other cases, with the pernicious effect of encouraging dangerous business'.[71] The variance is so high in 1898 because the National Bank of Scotland reports a rise in net profits from £214,000 to £312,000. Its rate of return on equity for 1898 is 14.15%, whereas the mean for the rest of the banks is 9.42%. It is probable that this increase in profit is merely an accounting illusion.

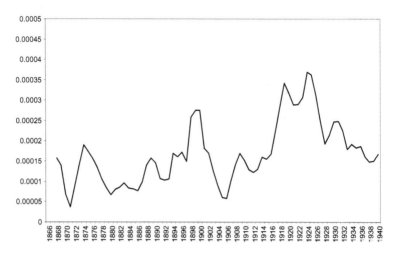

Figure 1.1 Variance of returns on equity

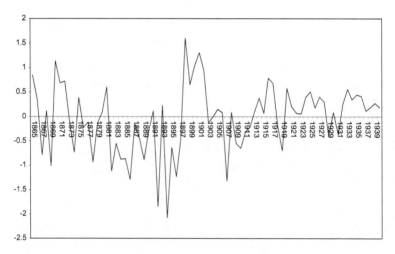

Figure 1.2 Skewness of returns on equity

The upward trend in the variance is broken by a four year period (1903–1906) where variance remains at a low level. However, after this period, there is an upward trend continuing until 1925. This suggests that some banks were gradually moving towards riskier profiles. This in turn suggests that some banks may have been engaging in opportunism.

After 1925, the trend in the graph is downwards. It is interesting to note that during the extremely unstable environment of the early 1930s, the variance measure falls. This adds weight to the claim made above that the variance measure would not be affected by economic conditions. It is argued in the next section that the fall in risk after 1925 was due to a new regulatory regime (introduced under the auspices of Montagu Norman) which constrained the ability of banks to engage in opportunism and encouraged banks to adopt similar risk-return profiles, thus moving banks to a pooling equilibrium.

The skewness of the rates of return distribution is shown in Figure 1.2. The skewness of the distribution increases after the move to limited liability and it does not decrease to low levels until the 1920s and 1930s. This again suggests that some banks were engaging in opportunism. The next section postulates that the low level of skewness after 1920 was due to the regulatory regime introduced by Montagu Norman which encouraged banks to adopt similar risk-return profiles, thus moving banks to a pooling equilibrium.

The traditional view of Scottish and English banking in the period 1880 to 1914 is that banks were very conservative. Capie and Mills[72] present evidence which argues that this was not the case. Furthermore, Munn[73] states that 'the traditional view that this was an era when bankers lent only short-term to well established customers is highly misleading'. The findings of this paper suggest that banks did not act in a conservative fashion, rather they engaged in opportunism by increasing the risks they took.

Table 1.3 presents further evidence which suggests that banks engaged in opportunism. Once banks move away from an unlimited liability status, capital acts as a constraint upon banks engaging in opportunism because bank failure means that shareholders lose their funds. However,

Table 1.3 Average equity/deposit ratio for Scottish banks 1865–1900

	Equity capital/total deposits (%)
1865	20.3
1870	19.5
1875	19.1
1880	19.7
1885	18.6
1890	16.5
1895	16.4
1900	15.7

Source: Bank annual reports.

as the equity/deposits ratio falls, banks have greater incentives to engage in riskier ventures.[74] Therefore, banks have incentives to reduce their equity/deposits ratio as this gives them greater ability to make risky advances.

The evidence presented in this section suggests that there was an increase in instability in Scottish banking after the move to limited liability, and this increase was due to banks not being constrained or restrained from engaging in opportunism. Figures 1.1 and 1.2 suggest that there was an institutional change which occurred around 1925 that led to a substantial reduction in risk-taking in the Scottish banking system. In the next section, it is argued that the institutional change which took place was the introduction of bank regulation and supervision.

V

It is commonly accepted that the Bank of England did not monitor or supervise commercial banks prior to the 1940s.[75] This paper, using evidence gathered from the Bank of England archives, suggests that Scottish and English banks were regulated and monitored from the early 1920s, and that this explains the reduction in banking instability post 1925.

After the Barings crisis, it is noteworthy how the Bank (with some Treasury pressure being brought to bear, notably from Chancellor Goschen) recognised its role as a monitor of the banking system. From 1891/92, according to the Bank's archives, the London Joint Stock banks and country banks were required to furnish the Bank with detailed monthly statements of their position.[76] Under Goschen's influence, the Bank also required banks to hold larger reserves.[77] The average liquid reserve ratio for the Scottish banking system is shown in Table 1.4.

Table 1.4 Average liquid assets/total assets ratio for Scottish banks 1865–1900

Liquid assets/total assets (%)		Liquid assets/total assets (%)	
1865	12.8	1905	19.3
1870	13.6	1910	20.1
1875	14.0	1915	21.8
1880	17.2	1920	21.7
1885	16.1	1925	20.3
1890	20.1	1930	19.9
1895	19.2	1935	20.0
1900	20.1	1940	24.4

Source: Bank annual reports.

In 1918, a Treasury committee passed a law requiring all banks, by statute, to register as banks, submit an audited balance sheet in a standardised form, and publish a statement at the end of each month again in a standardised form, signed by a qualified officer of the bank.[78] Therefore, by 1920, there was a formal monitoring structure which had essentially existed informally from 1891. The Bank's archives furnish little evidence of close monitoring of commercial bank's advances and investments. The monitoring which existed prior to 1920 was superficial in that the information obtained from monitoring would be of little use in ascertaining a bank's risk position. After World War One, there is evidence suggesting that if the Bank believed that a commercial bank was behaving in an opportunistic way, it would examine in detail its advances. An example of this occurred in June 1918 when Cox and Co. was asked by the Bank for the details of their overdrafts and loans.[79] Having ascertained that Cox and Co. was engaged in ventures which were too risky for banking prudence, the Bank used its powers of moral suasion to "encourage" Cox and Co. to increase its capital level and to engage in less risky areas.[80]

From 1920–1944, the Governor of the Bank was an astute central banker called Montagu Norman. He recognised, explicitly, the role of the Bank (backed by the government) as LOLR.[81] He was also aware of the moral hazard problem, and how the increase in bank size which was taking place exacerbated the moral hazard problem. For instance, in 1925, Norman said, 'Unless I am greatly mistaken, these persistent ramifications of the Clearing banks – which are already unwieldy in size – will in the long run bring more trouble than profit'.[82]

In 1925, Norman realised that a particular bank amalgamation imposed greater risk on the banking system because the Bank acted as a LOLR.[83] Norman's grasp of the Bank's duty as LOLR and the resultant moral hazard problem was to lead the Bank to monitor banks more intensely and use the power of moral suasion more powerfully and frequently to regulate banks.[84] It was Norman's resolute belief that 'a Central Bank should have power to examine banks which come to the Central Bank for credits and assistance'.[85]

During the Norman era, banks still had to provide monthly breakdowns of their balance sheets. However, as is evident from the Bank's archives,[86] especially from the late 1920s onwards, there was increased monitoring by means both of the annual informal interview which Norman had with the General Managers/directors of the major banks, and the 'routine reports' from the Chairmen of the clearing banks.[87] Among items discussed at these interviews were advances, investments, cash ratios, and rates on deposits/loans, capital and dividends. Norman would also suggest directions in which the particular banks should move. What was deemed prudent and safe banking was entirely at the discretion of the Bank; although at this time the Bank did have some stated policies such as banks not offering savings accounts, banks not participating in industry, and a desire to keep rates on bank advances low.[88]

Also, from the early twenties, there was clear policy on bank amalgamations. This was to stop what Norman called the 'unwieldy growth of commercial banks'.[89] He did however encourage the amalgamation of fragile banks with strong banks. For example, when William Deacon's was in trouble, its take-over by the Royal Bank of Scotland was encouraged by Norman.[90] Norman, in these circumstances, acted as an 'introduction agency' and 'persuader'.[91] Furthermore, he encouraged banks to be less involved in overseas loans or investments. He actively resisted the acquisition of foreign banks by the large clearing banks[92] because he believed that there was no cxcuse for extensions abroad – it was just a case of greed and megalomania on the part of banks.[93] Norman, like his grandfather G. W. Norman, had a huge distrust of banks engaging in overseas business.[94] Finally, he firmly believed in the separation of investment and commercial banking.[95]

It is argued here that the reduction in risk in the Scottish banking system after 1925 was due to Norman's regulatory style. He combined intensive monitoring with a high degree of moral suasion encouraging banks to hold safer loan portfolios, to lower rates on advances/deposits, and to increase capital. For example, the average capital/deposits ratio for Scottish banks in 1920 was 6.84%. By 1930, this figure had increased to 12.01%. It appears that under Norman's influence, the Scottish banks increased their capital levels. Although these levels were still well below the pre-war levels, the virtual doubling of capital ratios was a significant achievement.[96] How successful or how powerful was the use of moral suasion? Certainly, there were instances when Norman suggested a particular course of action and it was ignored, but when the course of action was vital to banking stability, Norman 'fought tough'. In 1938, the British Overseas Bank Limited (owned primarily by William Deacon's Bank Ltd, the Union Bank of Scotland Ltd and the Prudential Assurance Company Ltd.) had advanced a series of risky loans on the Continent and hadn't provided for any exchange rate risk. Norman asked Gairdner (chairman of BOB Ltd.) and the main shareholders to increase the capital of the bank. Norman was not interested in BOB Ltd. per se, but in the fact that two major clearing banks were the shareholders of a risky overseas trade bank. After much discussion and many threats, the two clearing banks gave up their ownership.[97]

On 8 April 1925, Norman, at a Committee of Treasury meeting, stated that if any bank disobeyed the Bank with regards to amalgamation policy, then that bank would not be entitled to support from the Bank, nor to recognition of its paper as prime for the purpose of discount, security or otherwise.[98] As the holder of the ultimate reserve and as the main player in the money market, the Bank of England had great power over commercial banks. If commercial banks didn't go along with the Bank's 'suggestions', then they were to be punished in this way.

It could be argued that the Scottish banking system was, to a certain extent, insulated from the moral suasion of Norman. The same could be said about English regional banks since Norman tended to focus upon the 'Big 5' due to their importance. However, he did realise that the stability of the regional banks was important and the Scottish banks were therefore subject to moral suasion. For example, the main Scottish banks all had to contribute to the bailout fund for the Anglo-South American Bank.[99] This was the first occasion Scottish banks had been asked to contribute to a bailout fund as they had not contributed to the Barings or Yorkshire Penny Bank bailouts. This and other evidence presented in this section suggests that the Scottish banking system was not overly insulated from the moral suasion of the Governor.

VI

It has been argued here that the move to limited liability banking in Scotland was made possible by the establishment of the Bank of England as a lender of last resort. The implication of this paper for the free banking school is that a free banking system with freedom to incorporate will be unstable, whereas a free banking system with a requirement of unlimited liability will be stable and not require government intervention. This finding agrees with Horwitz and Bodenhorn[100] who argue that a free banking system may require banks to possess unlimited liability.

The rise in instability which occurred after the move to limited liability was halted by the regulatory regime introduced by Montagu Norman. This regime may have been one of the reasons why the UK did not experience a banking crisis during the Great Depression. However, further research is required into this area. The implication of this paper for the recent banking crises across the developed and developing world is that the deregulation of banking systems may be one of the principal causes of banking instability.

Notes

* The author would like to express gratitude to Henry Gillet and the staff of the Bank of England Archives, and the staff at the University of Glasgow Archives. Thanks also go to the Bank of Scotland, Clydesdale Bank and the Royal Bank of Scotland for permission to access their material contained within the University of Glasgow Archives. The paper has benefited from comments made by Sheila Dow, Frank Geary, Charlie Hickson, Donal M Killop, Charles Munn, Gavin Reid, Anne-Louise Statt, Lawrence White and participants at the Scottish Economic Society conference, Glasgow, 1998. Financial support was provided by the Institute of Economic Affairs and Queen's University Belfast. Any remaining errors are the author's own.

1 L. H. White, *Free Banking in Britain: Theory, Experience and Debate 1800–1845* (London, 1995[1984]); K. Dowd, 'Option Clauses and the Stability of a Laissez Faire Monetary System', *Journal of Financial Services Research*, 1 (1988); M. N. Rothbard, 'The Myth of Free Banking in Scotland', *Review of Austrian Economics*, 2 (1988); J. L. Carr, S. Glied and G. F. Mathewson, 'Unlimited Liability and Free Banking in Scotland: A Note', *Journal of Economic History*, 49 (1989); T. Cowen and R. Kroszner, 'Scottish Banking before 1845: A Model for Laissez-faire?', *Journal of Money, Credit and Banking*, 21 (1989); L. J. Sechrest, 'Free Banking in Scotland: A Dissenting View', *Cato Journal*, 10 (1991); S. C. Dow and J. Smithin, 'Free Banking in Scotland, 1695–1845', *Scottish Journal of Political Economy*, 39 (1992); L. T. Evans and N. C. Quigley, 'Shareholder Liability Regimes, Principal-Agent Relationships, and Banking Industry Performance', *Journal of Law and Economics*, 35 (1995); J. A. Gherity, 'The Option Clause in Scottish Banking, 1730–65: A Reappraisal', *Journal of Law and Economics*, 38 (1995).

2 G. A. Selgin, 'Legal Restrictions, Financial Weakening, and the Lender of Last Resort', *Cato Journal*, 9 (1989), p. 456.

3 O. E. Williamson, *The Economic Institutions of Capitalism* (New York, 1985).

4 A. A. Alchian and S. Woodward, 'The Firm is Dead, Long Live the Firm', *Journal of Economic Literature*, 26 (1988).

5 W. Bagehot, 'Limited Liability in Banking – I', *The Economist* (May 1862), in *The Collected Works of Walter Bagehot* (London, 1976), p. 394.

6 One method to assure depositors of ex post contractual performance is the concept of brand name capital or charter value. However, in a finite horizon world, brand name capital or charter value have zero value in the last period of the contractual relationship and hence, in every preceding period due to the process of backwards induction. See R. S. Demsetz, M. R. Saidenberg and P. E. Strahan, 'Banks With Something to Lose: The Disciplinary Role of Franchise Value', *Federal Reserve Bank of Minneapolis Quarterly Review*, Winter (1996); G. Gorton, 'Bank Regulation When Banks and Banking Are Not the Same', *Oxford Review of Economic Policy*, 10 (1994). Also see B.

Klein, 'The Competitive Supply of Money', *Journal of Money, Credit and Banking*, 6 (1974).

7 S. G. Checkland, *Scottish Banking A History, 1695–1973* (Glasgow, 1975), p. 204.

8 A. W. Kerr, *Scottish Banking During the Period of Published Accounts 1865–1896* (London, 1898), p. 108.

9 Checkland, *Scottish Banking A History*, p. 275.

10 Ibid. p. 204.

11 Ibid. pp. 95, 204, 248, 275.

12 R. H. Campbell, 'Edinburgh Bankers and the Western Bank of Scotland', *Scottish Journal of Political Economy* (1955).

13 Checkland, *Scottish Banking A History*, p. 192.

14 C. W. Munn, *Clydesdale Bank: The First One and Fifty Years* (Glasgow, 1988), p. 39.

15 S. Woodward, 'Limited Liability in the Theory of the Firm', *Journal of Institutional and Theoretical Economics*, 141 (1985).

16 C. W. Munn, *The Scottish Provincial Banking Companies 1747–1864* (Edinburgh, 1981), p. 159.

17 Ibid. p. 160.

18 Woodward, 'Limited Liability in the Theory of the Firm'.

19 'Banks and Limitation of Liability', *Economist*, 25 October 1879 – reprinted in T. E. Gregory, *Select Statutes, Documents and Reports Relating to British Banking, 1832–1928* (London, 1929), pp. 297–300.

20 Munn, *Clydesdale Bank*, p. 15.

21 Ibid. p. 39.

22 The Banking Co-partnership Act (1826) required equity holders in English banks to retain liability up to three years after selling their share. See J. W. Gilbart (1828) "A Practical Treatise on Banking" quoted in P. L. Cottrell and B. L. Anderson, *Money and Banking in England: The Development of the Banking System 1694–1914* (London, 1974), p. 272.

23 Checkland, *Scottish Banking A History*, p. 467.

24 Ibid. p. 468.

25 Ibid. p. 480.

26 Figure calculated with data from T. Liesner, *One Hundred Years of Economic Statistics* (London, 1989) and B. R. Mitchell, *Abstract of British Historical Statistics* (London, 1962).

27 Share prices taken at end of January 1878 from the *Investors' Monthly Manual*.

28 Munn, *Clydesdale Bank*, p. 14.

29 M. D. Bordo, H. Rockoff and A. Redish, 'A Comparison of the Stability and Efficiency of the Canadian and American Banking Systems, 1870–1925', *Financial History Review*, 3 (1996).

30 Munn, *The Scottish Provincial Banking Companies*, p. 85.

31 S. G. Checkland, 'Banking History and Economic Development: Seven Systems', *Scottish Journal of Political Economy*, 15 (1968); Checkland, *Scottish Banking A History*; C. W. Munn, 'The Origins of the Scottish Note Exchange', *Three Banks Review*, 107 (1975); C. W. Munn, 'The Development of Joint-Stock Banking in Scotland, 1810–1845', in A. Slaven and D. H. Aldcroft (eds), *Business, Banking and Urban History* (Edinburgh, 1982);

26 John D. Turner

C. W. Munn, 'Review of White (1984)', *Business History*, 27 (1985), *Economic History Review*, 38 (1985).
32 J. Viner, *Studies in the Theory of International Trade* (Clifton, 1975), p. 243.
33 Checkland, *Scottish Banking A History*; Munn, 'The Development of Joint-Stock Banking in Scotland'; Munn, 'Review of White (1984)'; Tyson, 'Review of White (1984)'; Dow and Smithin, 'Free Banking in Scotland'.
34 C. A. E. Goodhart, *The Evolution of Central Banks* (Cambridge, MA and London, 1988), p. 8.
35 Munn, *Clydesdale Bank*, p. 15.
36 25+26 Vict. c. 89.
37 J. Clapham, *The Bank of England: A History* (London, 1944), Vol. 2, p. 306.
38 White, *Free Banking in Britain*, p. 50–51.
39 Evans and Quigley, 'Shareholder Liability Regimes'.
40 A. J. Wilson, *Banking Reform: An Essay on Prominent Dangers and the Remedies They Demand* (London, 1879), p. 77.
41 Kerr, *Scottish Banking During the Period of Published Accounts*, p. 155.
42 Clapham, *The Bank of England*, Vol. 2, p. 406.
43 Wilson, *Banking Reform*, p. 69.
44 W. F. Crick and J. E. Wadsworth, *A Hundred Years of Joint Stock Banking* (London, 1936), p. 32.
45 Ibid. p. 33.
46 42&43 Vict. c. 76.
47 'The Scotch Banks and the Limitation of Liability' in *The Banker's Magazine*, 40 (1880), pp. 899–903.
48 A. W. Kerr, *History of Banking in Scotland* (London, 1908), p. 308.
49 J. A. Wenley, 'On the History and Development of Banking in Scotland', *Journal of the Institute of Bankers*, 3 (1882).
50 'The Scotch Banks and the Limitation of Liability' in *The Banker's Magazine*, p. 902.
51 Evans and Quigley, 'Shareholder Liability Regimes'.
52 Wenley, 'On the History and Development of Banking in Scotland', p. 141.
53 Clapham, *The Bank of England*; M. Collins, *Money and Banking in the UK: A History* (London, 1988); F. W. Fetter and D. Gregory, *Monetary and Financial Policy in Nineteenth Century Britain* (Dublin, 1973); T. Ogden, *The Development of the Role of the Bank of England as a Lender of Last Resort*, Ph.D. dissertation (City University, 1988).
54 Fetter and D. Gregory, *Monetary and Financial Policy*, p. 25.
55 In a memo, dated 10 October 1931, contained in the Bank of England Archive (BoE) C48/68 (Banking Practice), the Bank's view was that if the ASAB was allowed to fail, it would have shook confidence in British banking institutions, leading quite possibly to runs on smaller banks with repercussions even on the most powerful.
56 W. Bagehot, 'Lombard Street' in *The Collected Works of Walter Bagehot* (London, 1976 [1873]), p. 133.
57 Alchian and Woodward, 'The Firm is Dead, Long Live the Firm', p. 71.
58 Interestingly, Munn, *Clydesdale Bank*, p. 85 points out that 'the early practice of the board authorizing every share transfer ceased in 1882'.
59 J. J. Knox, *A History of Banking in the United States* (New York, 1903).

60 C. A. E. Goodhart, *The Evolution of Central Banks*; C. A. E. Goodhart and D. Schoenmaker, 'Should the Functions of Monetary Policy and Banking Supervision Be Separated?', *Oxford Economic Papers*, 47 (1995).

61 Checkland, *Scottish Banking A History*, p. 486; Munn, *Clydesdale Bank*, pp. 144–45.

62 Checkland, *Scottish Banking A History*.

63 E. A. Boehm, *Prosperity and Depression in Australia 1887–1897* (London, 1971), pp. 211–213.

64 W. Bagehot, 'Unfettered Banking', *The Saturday Review* (November 1856) in *The Collected Works of Walter Bagehot* (London, 1976); W. Bagehot, 'The Safest Bank', *The Economist* (April, 1857) in *The Collected Works of Walter Bagehot* (London, 1976); Bagehot, 'Lombard Street'.

65 R. Sylla, 'Early American Banking: The Significance of the Corporate Form', *Business and Economic History*, 14 (1985); White, *Free Banking in Britain*.

66 The rate of return on equity is defined as net profits divided by capital plus shareholders' reserves.

67 C. R. Hickson and J. D. Turner, 'The Development of the Early Banking Firm and the Evolution of Banking Regulation', *Queen's University manuscript*.

68 D. M. Kreps, *Microeconomic Theory* (New York, 1990), chapter 17.

69 I thank an anonymous referee for pointing this out.

70 Checkland, *Scottish Banking A History*, p. 520.

71 Kerr, *Scottish Banking During the Period of Published Accounts*, p. 12.

72 F. H. Capie and T. C. Mills, 'British Bank Conservatism in the Late 19th Century', *Explorations in Economic History*, 32 (1995).

73 Munn, *Clydesdale Bank*, p. 84.

74 Alchian and Woodward, 'The Firm is Dead'.

75 J. Fforde, *The Bank of England and Public Policy, 1941–1958* (Cambridge, 1992), pp. 758–59.

76 BoE G16/1 (Historical Index of Bank of England Courts). According to Clapham, *The Bank of England*, Lidderdale suggested the use of interviews as a supervisory tool after the Barings crisis.

77 Goschen made a proposal in 1891/92 entitled '£1 note issue and the reserve of gold, 1891/92' – BoE G16/1.

78 BoE C40/79 (Banking Practice – Registration of Banks).

79 BoE C46/129 (Cox and Company).

80 BoE C46/129.

81 BoE G1/9 (Governor's Correspondence on Bank Amalgamations), memo dated 10 August 1925; a letter received and endorsed by Norman on 15 February 1923; and a confidential draft prepared by Norman regarding the amalgamation of the Colonial Bank, the Anglo-Egyptian Bank and the National Bank of South Africa.

82 BoE G1/9 – in a letter dated 18 June 1925.

83 BoE C40/79 – memo dated 10 August 1925.

84 BoE G1/9 – Norman believed it was a central bank's duty to make sure commercial banks behaved in a proper fashion.

85 H. Clay, *Lord Norman* (London, 1957), p. 283.

86 BoE G1/9, G1/10, G1/11 (Governor's Correspondence on Bank Amalgamations). For example, on a memo dated 4 December 1929, there is recorded

some of the discussion between Norman and Sir Christopher Needham (Chairman of District Bank) on the outlook regarding the District's
investments.

87 Clay, *Lord Norman*, pp. 276–78.
88 BoE C40/48 – memo dated 4/11/1932.
89 BoE G1/9 (letter from Chancellor to Norman dated 3/3/24 outlining government's wishes) – the main three Scottish banks (Commercial, Royal and
Union) could amalgamate with any bank in the UK except one of the 'Big 5'
(i.e. Midland, Lloyds, Barclays, Westminster and National Provincial). The
rest of the Scottish banks could amalgamate with the 'Big 5'.
90 BoE G1/10 – Amalgamations – letter dated 4/12/29 to Needham.
91 BoE G1/11 – Amalgamations – 1/8/35 correspondence with Needham.
92 Clay, *Lord Norman*, p. 280.
93 BoE G1/9 – in a letter dated 15/2/1923.
94 Clay, *Lord Norman*, p. 6.
95 Ibid. p. 58.
96 In 1910, the average capital / deposits ratio was 17.31%.
97 BoE C48/128 – the two clearing banks were William Deacon's Bank and
Union Bank of Scotland.
98 BoE G1/9 – extracts from minutes of Committee of Treasury dated Wed 8
April 1925.
99 BoE C48/68 Anglo-South American Bank – minutes of meeting of the
Credit Committee 23/9/31. The Royal Bank, Bank of Scotland, Commercial
Bank and National all had to contribute to the bailout fund.
100 S. Horwitz and H. Bodenhorn, 'A Property Rights Approach to Free Banking', *Journal des Economistes et des Etudes Humaines*, 5 (1994).

Postscript

This article resulted in a body of work published in the early 2000s exploring the role of unlimited and extended liability regimes in banking. Skin in the game in the form of extended shareholder liability made for stable banking. Little did we know that eight years after this *Journal of Industrial History* article was published, the global financial system would come crashing down and Western governments would employ extraordinary measures to rescue their banking systems.

The global financial crisis of 2008 resulted in Turner writing *Banking in Crisis: The Rise and Fall of British Banking Stability, 1800 to the Present*. This book was published in 2014 by Cambridge University Press and in 2015 it won the Wadsworth Prize for Business History.

His innovative study was the first to tell the story of the rise and fall of British banking stability over the past 200 years. Using a new approach to measuring banking instability, he argued that there have only been two major banking crises in Britain over the past two centuries – the crises of 1825–6 and 2007–8. Although there were episodic bouts of instability in the interim, the banking system was crisis free. *Banking in Crisis* grappled with two questions: why was the British banking system stable for such a long time? And, why did the British banking system implode in 2008? In answering these questions, Turner explored the long-run evolution of bank capital, the Bank of England's role, bank regulation and bank rescues. In his book, he concluded that to prevent a future banking collapse, we needed to learn from history and hold bank shareholders accountable. These were themes initially developed in his *Journal of Industrial History* article over two decades ago.

Chapter 2

The commercial banking industry and its part in the emergence and consolidation of the corporate economy in Britain before 1940

Peter Wardley

'He did not think the banks had yet explored the enormous possibilities of mechanical methods. He thought the counter work at English banks was about as efficient as they could ever get, but he was suspicious as to whether they were as up to date behind the counter. He could see the banks of the future as possessing physical bodies of wonderfully contrived mechanism, almost everything of routine being done by machinery with the brains for the personal convenience of customers, and scientific conditions of control, a great civil service with a high tradition of public service, with opportunities for development and employment of many different talents. On the other hand, it was conceivable they might develop into mere money making machines.'

> John Maynard Keynes, 'The future opportunities of the bank official'; presented at the Cambridge Centre of the Institute of Banking; reported in the *Cambridge Daily News*, 15 October 1927; and, reprinted as 'Mr J. M. Keynes on banking services' in the *Journal of the Institute of Banking*, November 1927, vol. xlviii, p. 497.

Banks engage in business which is intended to organise the profitable production of financial services and, like other privately-owned firms in a market economy, employ capital and labour to achieve this objective. Furthermore, as in other companies, it is within banks that more efficient combinations of capital and labour generate productivity growth. However, it has to be admitted that among banking historians, though usually not those who have written histories of banks, investigations of business structure, employment patterns, work organisation, labour relations and technological choice are notable usually for their omission. Nevertheless, these features of commercial banks, despite previous neglect, do have a wider significance for economists and economic historians and challenge a number of well-established historiographic prejudices.

Although banks are often treated as a special case, perhaps largely because their products are intangible, if not magical, to some observers, an investigation of bank organisation and performance can shed light on some often neglected aspects of modern economic growth. Three inter-related themes are highlighted here which suggest that the development of modern commercial banks can reveal significant but underappreci-ated facets of this vitally important phenomenon. These three themes, which are discussed in the context of British commercial banking before 1939, recognise: first, the relative importance of the services in a modern economy, for which banking here stands as representative of that general class of activity; second, the functional significance of the financial sec-tor and its relationship with other sectors of a modern economy; and, third, the consolidation of banks as large corporations which developed organisational structures adapted for the performance of banking activity in dynamic circumstances. While the third theme, which prompts ques-tions about the consolidation, structure and organisation of the largest English commercial banks, receives the major attention here the other two themes are indicated to locate its proper context and insist upon its more general significance.

The contribution of service sector activity to the process of modern economic growth has only recently begun to receive attention from economists and economic historians commensurate with its relative con-tribution to economic activity.[1] Typically it has been assumed that the industrial sector, and manufacturing in particular, has pride of place in the process of economic growth frequently, and significantly, referred to as the 'Industrial Revolution'. Nevertheless, the close association between sustained modern economic growth and the positive contribution of the services to productivity growth over the last century suggests that concen-tration on manufacturing leaves more than half the story untold, be it for an individual economy such as the United Kingdom,[2] or for international comparative perspectives.[3] Furthermore, the relationship between this process and the development of the large corporation, its key institutional determinant, alongside the state, suggests a complex and significant inter-connection between the development of big business on the one hand and structural change and economic development on the other.[4]

Second, and as indicated recently by Levine,[5] the significance and form of the financial sector for economic growth is a contentious issue: for some the financial system plays a crucial role, allowing the mobili-zation and direction of capital, whereas others regard its importance as either exaggerated or insignificant and barely worthy of mention.[6] One of the crucial tests for champions of the former proposition is the contrast between the British and German banking systems, which are held to exemplify the market-based and the bank-based financial systems, respectively. It has been often suggested that in the late nineteenth and early twentieth century the German bank-based financial system generated more rapid industrial growth than the British market-based system. But a conclusive demonstration of this proposition has proved elusive and the conclusions of more recent investigations, which have drawn on detailed archival research indicate that the English banking system more closely resembled most other European systems than did the German. Moreover, the differences between these two systems appear much more striking in the pages of the banking manuals, and subsequent economic history textbooks, than they would have been to the bankers who operated in either system.[7] It also has to be admitted that the rhetoric of the bankers themselves, rather than their practice, may have contributed greatly to this comparative assessment.

The third theme is the emergence of complex, large-scale industrial corporations which collectively comprise the corporate economy, conventionally defined in terms of the activities of the modern business enterprise in the industrial and extractive sectors.[8] This is another contentious issue and one where, yet again, the British example often does not escape unfavourable comparison.[9] Chandler's most recent work suggests a taxonomy designed to illustrate international comparative analysis of the relationship between economic performance and the emergence of the modern industrial enterprise; this classifies the United States as 'competitive managerial capitalism', Germany as 'co-operative managerial capitalism', and the British system as 'personal capitalism'.[10] For Britain, because of the persistence of personal capitalism, the consequences were deleterious as economies of scale or scope remained unexploited. *Scale and Scope* contains an oft-quoted paragraph which serves to crystallize the key elements of this managerial response which is taken to underpin the development of modern business enterprise and the Corporate Economy:

> The first was an investment in production facilities large enough to exploit a technology's potential economies of scale or scope. The second was an investment in a national and international marketing and distributing network, so that the volume of sales might keep pace with the new volume of production. Finally, to benefit fully from these two kinds of investment the entrepreneurs also had to

invest in management: they had to recruit and train managers not only to administer the enlarged facilities and increased personnel in both production and distribution, but also to monitor and co-ordinate those two basic functional activities and to plan and allocate resources for future production and distribution. It was this three-pronged investment in production, distribution, and management that brought the modern industrial enterprise into being.[11]

These managerial responses are considered later, with specific reference to English commercial banking, but some general notes of caution should be identified immediately. On this side of the Atlantic, Chandler's verdict has been scrutinised with admiration but not a little scepticism because of the many facets of economic development which appear to have been banished from its ambit.[12] Chandler has also not escaped criticism back in the U. S. A.[13] Furthermore, a recent investigation of European big business by Cassis, which encompasses firms located in the United Kingdom, correctly emphasises the relatively large scale, longevity, profitability and overall success of large British companies.[14]

Recent research has also demonstrated that at the beginning of the twentieth century, British firms, although frequently described as relatively small and managerially challenged,[15] were much larger than they have been portrayed.[16] The adoption of estimated market value as a standard comparator indicates that in 1905, apart from a handful of major American corporations, the largest British and U. S. manufacturing companies fell within a very similar size range. Moreover, when this comparison is extended to *all* companies in both economies, so that service-providing companies are considered, rather than just industrial corporations, the much remarked upon difference in size between American and British companies disappears.[17] And English commercial banks figure prominently amongst these large service sector companies which are all too often overlooked in this context.

Concurrently, revisionist scrutiny has also been directed at the role of banks in the emergence of the British corporate economy, where they are customarily cast as neglectful and deficient suppliers of credit to industrial concerns.[18] While bankers have often been blamed for restricting industry's access to capital in the interwar period, when they faced particularly severe criticism for creating a barrier to organisational change or rationalisation,[19] a counterview suggests British banks were not systematically neglectful of industry's financial needs but the problems of the industrial sector were such they defied even the substantial resources, experience and clout of the English banks.[20] Unsurprisingly, this unfolding academic debate reflects the divergence of opinion held by contemporaries.[21] Whereas critics of the banking system, mainly commentators and politicians, insisted that the British economy, and especially the industrial sector, was being handicapped by its banking system, bankers themselves, and not a few industrialists, forthrightly rejected this opinion, arguing that banks met fully their responsibilities to shareholders, customers and employees.

Two major aspects of interwar banking history are discussed below to emphasise their importance as key institutions in the emergence of the corporate economy in Britain. First, the emergence and consolidation of the large English commercial banks and their significance among the ranks of Britain's largest companies is outlined briefly. Attention then moves to the internal features of the major banks to consider their nature, structure and organisation. This second theme highlights the significant emergence of explicit managerial structures which divorced control from ownership, manifested an explicitly hierarchical bureaucratic system and accommodated strategic, functional and operational capabilities. These new managerial structures fostered the implementation of policies designed to achieve at least the following interconnected objectives: organisational change; increased functional specialisation; financial innovation; technical change; and, the consolidation of an internal labour market. Two explicit features of the latter were a formal career ladder and a discriminatory employment policy. Taken together, these objectives demonstrate the recognition and deliberate shaping of corporate culture. In short, British banks adopted a new business strategy in the 1920s which both required significant managerial innovation and allocated the resources required to implement, supervise and control the achievement of that goal. Moreover, the determinants of this strategy were endogenous to the major British banks. Implementation of this new business strategy may have been timely, coinciding as it did with the onset of the Great Depression in Germany and the United States, but the economic difficulties which followed 1929 were an exogenous factor which further justified existing policy rather than a primary spur to change.

The scale of the English commercial banks can be indicated by a number of measures, including: market value; employment; number of branch offices; assets; deposits taken; advances provided; and, profits,[22] both declared and actual.[23] The size of British commercial banks, as indicated by market value and their rank order among Britain's largest companies, is shown in Table 2.1;[24] clearly, by 1905 Britain's largest banks qualified for inclusion among the ranks of international 'Big Business'. While consolidation of the United Kingdom banking system resulted in

Table 2.1 English commercial banks as big business: Market value of equity (£m.) and rank order of the English commercial banks *among* the largest British companies listed in *diminishing* size, by market value, in 1934/5 and 1904/5

	1934/5		1904/5	
	£m.	Rank	£m.	Rank
Midland Bank	58.2	(11)	11.6	(30)
Barclays Bank	54	(13)	9.1	
Lloyds Bank	43.8	(21)	14.1	(26)
Westminster Bank	38.7	(23)	7.8	(47)
National Provincial Bank	34.2	(26)	13.1	(27)
London and County Banking Company			9.8	(36)
Parr's Bank			7.1	(50)
Union of London & Smiths Bank,			8.5	(41)
Bank of England	53.7	(14)	44.5	(11)
Bank of Ireland	[IFS]		9.9	(35)

Source: P. Wardley (1991). 'The anatomy of big business: aspects of corporate development in the twentieth century', *Business History*, vol. 33, no. 2, pp. 268–296; Tables 2 and 3.

Notes: The Westminster Bank, as it became in 1923, was the result of many amalgamations which transformed the original London & Westminster Bank founded in 1834; these include two banks which appear above as independent banks in 1905: the London and County Bank (amalgamated in 1909) and Parr's Bank (1918). The Union of London and Smiths Bank was the third bank listed above in 1905 which was subsequently amalgamated; it became part of the National, Provincial & Union Bank in 1918, retitled in 1924 the National Provincial Bank. The Bank of England, the central bank for the United Kingdom, was privately owned by its shareholders, as was the Bank of Ireland which became the central bank of the Irish Free State (IFS) founded in 1922.

the primacy of the 'Big Five' by 1919,[25] it also significantly increased concentration in the banking system;[26] furthermore, as Table 2.1 shows, it also increased their relative standing in the national hierarchy of large companies.

The expansion of the Midland Bank, the largest of the 'Big Five', is demonstrated in Table 2.2 which highlights a number of significant features: the extent to which expansion had occurred before 1910; the growth which took place in the decade dominated by the First World War; the further consolidation of the 1920s; and, relative stasis in the decade before 1940. For the Midland Bank it is also significant not only that expansion after 1920 came from the opening of new offices, rather than from further amalgamation, but also that rationalisation occurred with the closure of over one hundred and fifty branches, largely where facilities were locally duplicated.[27] Like all its rivals, the Midland Bank engaged in an extensive, and expensive, building programme which saw

Table 2.2 Midland Bank expansion, 1880–1960

1) Balance sheet reports of paid-up capital, deposits, advances, bills and actual profits, £ millions:

	Capital paid up	Deposits	Advances	Bills	Actual profits
1880	0.3	2.0	1.3	0.6	0.06
1890	0.6	5.6	3.5	1.4	0.14
1900	2.5	37.8	19.8	4.1	0.58
1910	4.0	73.4	41.1	6.7	0.89
1920	10.9	371.8	189.7	57.7	4.2
1930	14.2	399.6	203.6	83.9	2.1
1939	15.2	496	221	n.a.	2.8
1950	15.2	1.392	344	n.a.	2.7
1960	24.2	1,709	759	n.a.	8.3

2) Staff employed, total number of branches and sub-branches open, and sources of change in stock of branches:

	Staff employed	Branches & sub-branches open	Branches added/Branches opened/Branches closed by amalgamation		
			(over previous decade)		
1890	350	45	8	16	–
1900	1,500	314	149	111	8
1910	3,691	689	247	135	3
1920	10,697	1,497	517	274	5
1930	13,192	2,100	–	691	91
1940	13,548	2,031	–*	126*	60*
1950	15,648	2,118	n.a.	n.a.	n.a.
1960	21,970	2,273	n.a.	n.a.	n.a.

Sources: W. F. Crick and J. E. Wadsworth, *A Hundred Years of Joint Stock Banking* (1958: 3rd. ed.: Hodder and Stoughton: London), pp. 326, 333, 347; A.R. Holmes and E. Green, *Midland: 150 years of banking* (1986: Batsford: London), pp. 323–326, 332–335, 339.

Notes: * Data only available for the quinquennium 1930–34.
n.a. not available.

the construction of new branches and re-location to new head offices near the Bank of England.[28]

Although the Midland Bank was the largest of the 'Big Five',[29] it was not untypical. Modest shifts in relative size apart,[30] the stability achieved by the 'Big Five' during the interwar years stands in marked contrast to the experience of, for example, the financial systems of Germany and the United States in the early 1930s. Nevertheless, despite similarities, each of the 'Big Five' had its own individual corporate culture. For example, with reference to organisational structure, the Midland is usually presented as the most centralised and Barclays the least.[31] However, this balance of centrifugal and centripetal tendencies was one of emphasis, or degree, and it would be all too easy to overstate differences between the banks. Strategy for each of the 'Big Five' banks was determined by senior executives at headquarters located in London. And, although greater or lesser latitude could be granted by executive officers to senior managers in the regions, there was relatively little difference in the central office functions undertaken at the respective headquarters of the 'Big Five'. This communality of practice with regard to managerial innovation was also enhanced by frequent and detailed exchange of information between senior bank officers; by contrast, little or nothing was revealed at such meetings about each bank's respective customers and their terms of business.

Here the managerial innovations and changes in accounting practices required to achieve bank amalgamation should not be underestimated, and neither should the contending sectional identities which evidenced a previous heritage. Naturally, the ensuing difficulties were probably most severe in a former head office rendered by amalgamation a mere branch. Even in the Midland, this process of internal consolidation was only completed a decade after the death, in 1919, of its architect, Sir Edward Holden.[32]

The corporate culture of each of the 'Big Five' was a result of the varied history of the bank itself. Each constituent bank acquired during the long, drawn-out process of growth by amalgamation brought with it its own idiosyncratic practices and customs. As Crick and Wadsworth point out, this proved to be an enduring problem:

> 'Time and again amalgamations had given rise to the necessity of removing acute differences of method which involved inefficiency and waste. Often it was found that systems of branch organisation and control had been shaped on different lines, and it was necessary to bring these systems into uniformity in order to secure the highest common factor of efficiency.'[33]

In the search for efficiency and internal uniformity each of the 'Big Five' banks introduced a number of managerial innovations; these included: the consolidation of managerial structures which permitted functional specialisation, both at the head office and in the individual branch; the development of internal labour markets; and, the introduction of new technology, which itself had major implications for the organisation, administration and operation of the major clearing banks. Many aspects of the labour process were transformed, with gender playing a significant role, such that the business culture of each of these organisations was reconstructed in the interwar period.

Corporate development and the organisation of English banks before 1939

Consolidation of the 'Big Five' required the development of clear management structures and a division of responsibilities between the head office and the branches. Much of this depended upon the transmission of high quality and relevant information: head office functions could be performed efficiently only if branches provided regular communication of appropriate standardized information; branches could act effectively only if the instructions issued from head office were regular, specific, and informed. New procedures were adopted, or old ones adapted, to ensure that the branch system worked under the supervision of the central office; it was, however, essential that these procedures, whatever their heritage, were formalised. Even where the necessary managerial structures were in place before the First World War, as in the case of the Midland Bank,[34] they were reassessed and recast according to new demands, circumstances and opportunities. As discussed below, mechanization was an instance of this.

This essential divide between head office and branch resulted in formal functional specialisation which can be illustrated by a model derived from a contemporary account of English banking methods written by Leonard le Marchant Minty.[35] The term "model" is not used by Minty, but it does seem apt as he generalises to produce an archetype representing the essential organisational features of the 'Big Five', even though each had its own characteristics and idiosyncrasies. It is probable that the Westminster Bank was probably the closest to this ideal type. Figure 2.1 illustrates the departmental structure of a head office. The titles of the various departments refer to the various departments and indicate both their functions and the extent of internal functional specialisation.[36] One department has been added to Minty's schema[37] – the Machinery Department, a very recent innovation, as demonstrated below.

Even before the First World War, 'Big Five' banks had installed 'Foreign' or 'Overseas' departments to undertake banking business external to the United Kingdom: Lloyds Bank's foreign department was established

Board Room:

Directors

Executive Offices:

Chairman
Managing Directors
Joint General Managers
Assistant General Managers

Functional departments:

Chief Accountant's Office	Legal Department
Branch Inspection Office	Premises Department
Chief Inspector's Office	Safe and Securities Department
Bill Office and Brokers' Loans	Intelligence Department
Stock Office	Staff Department
New Issues Office	Income Tax Department
The Coupon Office	Credit Information Department
Clearing Departments	Stationery Department
Branch Ledger Department	Machinery Department
Head Office Correspondence & Circulating Department	

Figure 2.1 Organizational structure, and functional specialization by department,
of the headquarters offices of an interwar British joint stock bank

Source: after L. le M. Minty, *English Banking Methods* (4th ed., London 1930).

in 1898,[38] the Midland's Foreign Banks Department by 1902.[39] True to
their distinctive histories and corporate cultures, organisation of this
facility varied by bank. Where the Midland Bank had a single centralized department, decentralisation determined that Barclays Bank's Chief
Foreign Branch was supplemented not only by provision in the West
End (Pall Mall, London) but also by Foreign branches in Manchester,
Liverpool, Bradford, and in 1927, Birmingham.[40] Like the Head Office,
foreign branches or departments also exhibited specialisation by function: Figure 2.2 indicates the sections which provided the international
banking services demanded by the customers of a 'Big Five' Bank.[41]
As a specific example of corporate enterprise, Minty highlighted here
the Midland's establishment in 1919 of a department to supervise its
branch banks on board Cunard's ocean liners.[42] Specialist sections were
also created to supervise transactions between branches overseas and
branches in England and even to advise on 'Enemy Debts' after World
War One. Interestingly, the foreign departments of a 'Big Five' bank
often provided a initial testing ground for the implementation of new

Functional departments:

Dealing Room	Foreign Bills for Collection
Telegraphic Transfer	Inland Bills
Currency Account	Securities
Sterling Accounts	
Cash or Clearing Department	Mail Transfers
Inland Payments	Correspondence Department

Commercial Credits "Inwards"
Commercial Credits "Outwards"

plus, specialist offices:

Enemy Debts Clearing Department
Cunard Office (Midland Bank)

Figure 2.2 Functional specialisation by department of a 'Foreign' or 'Overseas'
branch of an interwar British joint stock bank

Source: after L. le M. Minty (4th ed., London 1930) *English Banking Methods.*

methods and techniques, including machine accounting. By the 1920s, increasing demands on head office facilities and expansion of foreign business often required the relocation of the foreign branch to a separate but proximate location, increasing still further the necessity of a standardised managerial information system.

Although the determination of strategy and higher managerial functions were confined to the head office of a 'Big Five' bank, functional specialization was also to be found at the branches. By 1930 an average branch probably had about seven staff but the larger branches could have *circa* thirty staff, including: a manager; a sub-manager; an accountant; four or five cashiers; four or five ledger keepers; between ten and twelve other clerks; two juniors; six lady clerks; two messengers and a nightwatchman. Here, too, the physical layout of the branch coincided with the functions delivered. The public were served by cashiers at the counter; behind was the waste office which accepted cheques and recorded the details in waste books; then came the ledger office where debits and credits were entered to customer accounts; and, last in this progression through the branch, was the Day Book, a department which processed information provided by the Ledger Officer and recorded it in Ledger Books and produced the all important trial balance. Additionally, there would be a Correspondence Office, a Bills and Securities Office,

Figure 2.3 A traditional branch banking office – the Portishead branch of the National Provincial Bank at the beginning of the twentieth century. (*NatWest Group Archives*)

an Accountant's Office, where the returns to head office would be prepared, together with separate office accommodation for the Manager and Sub-Manager.[43]

It was the branch where most customers came into contact with the bank's staff. Only the most important clients had dealings with head office which scrutinised all major loans over a specified amount, below this stipulation a branch manager was allowed discretion. One important part of a branch's business was the search for new accounts and one financial innovation, the home safe, was introduced in the 1920s to attract new customers with relatively small surpluses. Business undertaken in many branches also changed significantly as cheques became much more heavily used in the 1920s and bills declined in relative importance. This shift in demand for bank services on the part of customers had major implications for the banks which faced a much heavier working load as a consequence and this was an additional stimulus to the search for cost cutting measures.

Figure 2.4 Machine banking in interwar Britain: the central banking hall at Lothbury after the mechanisation of the Westminster Bank's headquarter functions. (*NatWest Group Archives*)

While the branches delivered the bank's services to its customers, the various departments functioned in accordance with the policies laid down by senior managers who, in conjunction with the board of directors, determined strategy. The functional intermediaries, who played the essential role of overseeing the communication and implementation of policy, were the Bank Inspectors. In addition to their role of 'policing' the branches to ensure accounting efficacy and probity, the inspectors ensured that policy and procedure was understood and acted upon by each branch. It was probably the Inspectors who initially saw the potential, and recognised the necessity of introducing new methods which would enable the bank to operate more efficiently. The Machinery

Departments were closely linked and were eventually to be reabsorbed into the Inspection Departments. One important role usually played by the Inspection Department of a 'Big Five' bank was a regular review of the performance of individual staff members, this review informed decisions concerning promotion and salary increments which were essential features of the bank's internal labour market.

Internal labour markets

A substantial branch system directed by a centralized and specialist head office required a large number of employees and the development of internal labour markets; moreover, it required the development of a formal, standardised system to record the careers of all employees.[44] The 'Big Five' developed internal labour markets at least fifty years before economists drew attention to the consequences of this development.[45] In the context of a dual labour market, clearly the 'Big Five' provided 'primary' jobs designed to secure a stable labour force. Once admitted to a staff position through the limited 'port of entry', normally recruiting directly from school on the basis of examination performance, banks provided male staff with 'good' jobs: the rate of remuneration was relatively high; standard incremental pay scales offered protection against the vagaries of the market and arbitrary decisions of superiors; tenure was secure; pension rights were guaranteed; holidays entitlements and 'perks' were specified; and, for male entrants alone, a promotion ladder appeared to offer the opportunity to ascend to the summit of the managerial hierarchy. Furthermore, these contractual aspects were buttressed by a number of devices designed to foster a corporate culture; these included in-house staff magazines, social activities and sports clubs.

Trade unions often figure in the literature as important determinants of internal labour markets; however, although the banks tolerated or encouraged, perhaps less than enthusiastically the organisation of internal company-specific staff associations, the limited success of the Bank Officers Guild, which was registered as a trade union in 1920, suggests this factor was marginal, if not irrelevant, in this case. Similarly, high labour turnover, another reason sometimes cited by labour economists to account for an internal labour market, can also be discounted. However, there was one determinant that may have played a role here, though not one usually associated with the banking industry; internal labour markets are often associated with companies which are dynamic and exploit changing technology, which corresponds with the significance of mechanization ascribed below.

For banks, however, there was an obvious causal factor. It was particularly important for a bank to secure employees who exhibited specific personal qualities and characteristics including honesty, integrity and trust: theoretical issues associated with moral hazard and the principal-agent relationship are not difficult to identify in the banking industry. Moreover, not only were bank employees obliged to act so that they generated customer confidence when they appeared behind the bank counter or in the bank office, they were also expected to act as respectable and trustworthy individuals outside working hours, playing a responsible role in the local society.[46]

The 'Big Five' banks also developed discriminatory labour policies. By the 1930s female clerical staff also enjoyed tenure, incremental pay scales and, relative to other female workers, advantageous working conditions, but they received much lower rates of remuneration,[47] were subject to a marriage bar,[48] and faced a concrete rather than a glass ceiling, having no prospects for promotion to senior managerial or executive posts. Porters and messengers faced very restricted pay scales, sometimes age-related; however, gender discrimination continued even at this lower level in a bank's hierarchy as female cleaners and canteen workers received a lower, basic wage.

These internal market structures appear to illustrate an efficiency-orientated institutional response to the market forces generated by firm-specific jobs, training and technology as suggested by Williamson, Wachter, and Harris.[49] With the establishment of those parameters of the labour contract which could be explicitly specified to the satisfaction of both parties, given the realities of power relationships between management and employees, at least some of the costs of perpetual bargaining over the labour effort and turnover costs were reduced or eliminated.

Moreover, as the banks improved their screen processes, through the introduction of training courses, encouragement of examination success and, in particular, appraisal schemes, it became possible to encourage efficiency through the promotion of staff judged meritorious. Thus the effects of promotion, both effective and demonstrative, reduced the costs of monitoring and supervision and contributed to the development of an efficient internal labour market. Pay scales and promotion ladders not only encouraged staff to acquire the specific information and skills required to fulfil their current employment obligations but also ensured that staff had opportunities to develop specific training which would equip them to serve in senior posts (learning, at the very least, "sitting by Nellie"). Consequently, when acting in either a supervisory or policy-making capacity, managers would not only understand the nature of the job but they would also understand how and why it was done.

Although remuneration was paid to the job rather than on an assessment of individual performance, the 'Big Five' developed similar internal markets, each bank ensuring that training was a complement to the production of bank services and screening advancement for appropriate individuals according to specific criteria; such institutional relationships and arrangements, it has been suggested, 'may well be the most efficient apparatus for collecting and analysing data on individual performance'.[50] Although some of these institutional relationships already

Figure 2.5 "Then" and "Now". C. Sporn's cartoon refelecting changing attitudes to women employees. NATPROBAN (Autumn 1938), p. 77. (*NatWest Group Archives*)

had a long history by the outbreak of the First World War, many were relatively new, and probably the majority of these arrangements were disrupted by changes introduced in the 1920s. After 1928 mechanization was to transform many aspects of bank practice.

Mechanization, machine ledger keeping and centralization in English commercial banks

Although the telephone could be seen as the pioneering modern technology, many new techniques and gadgets were adopted in commercial offices, banks included, at the beginning of the twentieth century.[51] Alongside typewriters, besides steel filing cabinets, and under electric lighting, a range of new materials, products and techniques were to be found that supplemented novel adding machines introduced as the first mechanical aids to banking almost coincident with the outbreak of the First World War.

The major technical innovation of the interwar period introduced both at head offices and in the branches of the 'Big Five' was the introduction of accounting machines which allowed the posting, or data handling, of bank ledgers and customer statements, both commercial and personal. With accounting machines came standardization as their introduction transformed banking operations with the implementation of procedures designed to ensure all data handling (i.e. data collection, data presentation, data processing, data storage and data retrieval) were systematic and uniform. The specific machines preferred by an individual bank depended upon an assessment of the features supplied and the bank's requirements, but each of the 'Big Five' responded to rising costs and an increase in business, both the number of customers and transaction undertaken, by adopting this technology.

While this technology could be described as primitive and unwieldy from a vantage point at the end of the twentieth century, it was the "cutting-edge" technology of its day. Furthermore, in addition to being an essential step to technically superior systems, this technology, and the associated management information system created to utilise it, was a highly successful innovation provided the key-stone of the banks' operations for the next thirty years, when it was replaced by new management systems created to accommodate mainframe computers. For those who like to view the development of economies and businesses in terms equivalent to biological processes this sequence can be seen as an excellent example of punctuated equilibrium where a period of stasis is followed by one of rapid change after which stasis is restored, with the

Figure 2.6 'Our mechanised banks: the inspectors call', *Spread Eagle* (1930), p. 531. (*Barclays Bank Archives*)

possibility of a similar epoch of transition disturbing the new equilibrium at a later date.[52]

Detailed descriptions of the technology and assessments of the various machines appeared in the banking journals, particularly in the autumn of 1929 when this was a 'hot' topic. Full descriptions and technical details of neither the book-keeping systems nor the various machines is provided here, although the relevant manufacturers are indicated by

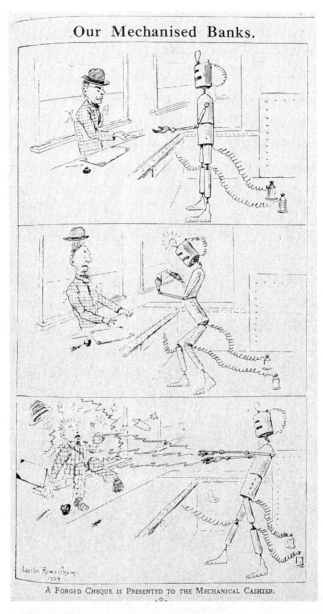

Figure 2.7 'Our mechanised banks: a forged cheque is presented to the mechanical cashier', *Spread Eagle* (1931), p. 283. (*Barclays Bank Archives*)

reference to a contemporary expert, assessing a decade of machine banking in an article published in 1938, who would have sympathised with
this omission:

> "It will be noticed that I have made no attempt to distinguish between
> methods of book-keeping in the proposed centralized book-keeping
> offices. It does not seem to me important for the moment to discuss
> whether the machines of the Burroughs, National Cash Register,
> Remington etc. companies are used, nor is this the place to argue
> the merits of these machines as against entirely different methods
> such as are utilized by punched-card machines of the Hollerith or
> Powers-Samas type."[53]

By the mid-1920s senior managers of the 'Big Five' held growing concerns about rising costs of production and control over the process of
production which gave rise to an interest in mechanization.[54] Although
the Midland Bank and the Westminster Bank were the most visible pros-
elytisers, reporting their progress in a 'Special Issue' of *The Banker*
(itself an unusual, if not unique, event) entitled 'Bank Mechanization'
in August 1929, the other large commercial banks were already inau-
gurating their own systems. By 1930 the 'Big Five' had all introduced
more or less complete systems of machine-book keeping and similar systems had been introduced at many of the London offices of the Colonial
banks. However, although the systems were complete, implementation
was largely restricted to Head Offices and larger branches. As implementation continued the minimum size of an economically viable machine
ledger branch fell from the initial estimate of 15 staff in 1928 to 12 in
1930,[55] and to 8 in 1933.[56] At this limit mechanization would have been
economic in only about half the branches of each of the 'Big Five' but
the scope for mechanization was enlarged by grouping smaller branches
together in a local clearing pool served by a single mechanized branch
which processed the records of the others.

Centralization,[57] as this was known at the Midland Bank, was implemented in December 1929 and discussed at a meeting of the Institute of
Banking Debating Society the following month. The star performer
at this session was H. L. Rouse (Assistant Chief Accountant at the
Midland Bank). Rouse reported the extent to which mechanization had
been introduced, with 73 branches converted to the new system, and
plans for a further 45 branches to be converted during 1930. The new
system already accommodated approximately 165,000 accounts and
catered for 7,000,000 postings a month; in all 325 machines had been

installed; 296 machines at Head Office and various large branches, plus 29 machines to cope with the work at months end and heavy periods. Rouse also reviewed branch expansion and the increase in employment in the Midland Bank since 1924 to indicate how mechanization allowed the substitution of female labour and capital for male staff with a consequent reduction in cost.[58]

Rouse also explained that although the proportion of women employed in the bank would increase, the promotion opportunities of newly recruited male clerks would improve and, from the bank's point of view, this would encourage the quality of male recruitment; the latter had been a recurrent cause for concern for the senior officers since mechanization had begun and it had only been made worse by the restraint on recruitment which followed the economic downturn after 1929. The allocation of mundane and repetitive tasks to female machine operatives would facilitate more rapid promotion of junior male staff 'to undertake such responsible tasks as the discounting of bills, cashiering, and security work'. He also pointed out that with this creation of two distinct categories of staff, with supervisory and clerical grades, British banks would more closely resemble Continental and American banks.[59]

Mechanization in the 'Big Five' even had an impact on popular culture, as reports of robotic bankers swept the national press when a machine accounting system was introduced at Lothbury, the head offices of the Westminster Bank, on 18 April 1933. This was accomplished only after a full appraisal of the Bank's existing system and its functional departments (see Figures 2.1 and 2.2) had been conducted to plan a comprehensive re-organisation of management structures and operations. This strategic view informed the detailed specification of the plan and drew upon experience gained in the mechanization of over a hundred branches and Threadneedle Street. Mechanized in February 1932, Threadneedle Street was the location of some head office functions, including the bank's training school. Once the decision had been taken to mechanize Lothbury, accounting machines were selected, after careful appraisal of the range of available models, and intensive six week training programmes were organised at the Bank's training school, which equipped head office staff with the skills required to operate the system to be implemented. After the event, this training, which had been followed by an ensuing period of practical experience in a mechanized branch, was recognised as being of 'enormous importance'.[60] Finally, the internal lay-out of Lothbury was reconstructed, section by section, to minimise disturbance to business (see Figure 2.4), according to plans drawn up the bank's architect to meet the following criteria:

'1   Every ledger and statement poster, and every control operator, has what is effect an office to himself including all the desk space and filing accommodation required for his work. He can, therefore, work in complete comfort, and no matter how much traffic there is in the gangways he cannot be incommoded.

2   All other machine operators have desks beside the machines of sufficient size for the work of sorting, etc., and ample gangways behind them so that they also can work in comfort.

3   All lighting has been specially designed so that any glare from the keys is avoided. The amount of light is ample and can be varied by each operator. There is a separate light for each machine.

4   Every machine has a separate fuse plug beside it with a cartridge fuse so that a fuse blowing affects only the particular machine and takes on a few seconds to replace.

5   Everything has been so arranged that the work flows forward from one stage to the next with the minimum amount of movement. Cross traffic has been avoided.

6   Very ample filing space of the most suitable design for the particular forms, etc., has been provided in the places most convenient for the work.'[61]

Careful specification of working conditions was matched by a close inspection of work undertaken by head office departments. After a detailed study of departmental organisation at Lothbury, work was reorganized so that: all possible work was mechanized; all work in mechanized departments which could not be mechanized was transferred to non-mechanized departments; the procedures of non-mechanized sections were changed so they integrated with those of mechanized sections; and, 'everyone in non-mechanized sections understood exactly the changes, if any, that machine accountancy would necessitate in their existing procedures'.[62]

Within a year of its original conception, and after six months of careful preparation for its execution, the changeover from the hand-written system to machine accounting at the Westminster Bank was achieved between the close of business on Easter Saturday and the next working day.[63]

Having illustrated the extent of managerial changes implemented in the 'Big Five' during the interwar period, there remains the question of its efficacy in producing cost reductions. The example of the Midland Bank will suffice, at least for the moment, to indicate the scale of economies achieved by mechanization, the associated influx of female staff and managerial reorganization in general. Six years after the initial implementation of mechanical ledger posting Rouse was able to refine his earlier estimate that two male clerks could be released for the cost of one female machine operator with more definite results: 'the actual figures show that for every two ledger-posting machines installed, 2.1 male clerks have been released and it has only been necessary to engage .5 female operators for every two ledger-posting machine installed'.[64] As female salaries (circa £150 p. a.) were half those of their male counterparts (circa £300 p. a.) this represented a significant saving in labour costs. As the ledger-posting machines cost in the order of £420 and had a life expectancy of about ten years, the total savings, after allowing for the cost of the capital equipment were far from insignificant. Contemporary estimates, based conservatively on Rouse's initial evaluation of staffing redeployment, suggested that the break-even point, after investment in all aspects of the system (i.e. including training, accommodation, sundry expenses etc.), would occur about two years after the installation of accounting machines. In crude terms, though, the saving achieved by the installation of each machine approximated to the salary of a male staff employee.

Overall, it would appear that by 1939, through the introduction of machine accounting the 'Big Five' had collectively made annual net savings on costs in excess of £1 million;[65] this was a reduction equivalent to about 7% of total labour charges and *circa* 3% of total costs. Although all the savings achieved through related managerial and employment changes are not included in this estimate, it does represent an initial, though approximate and admittedly conservative, financial estimate of the economies of scale achieved by the 'Big Five' through the operation of national branch banking systems supervised centrally from a head office.

However, mechanisation of British banking accomplished much beyond its cost cutting objective. In addition to the direct economic benefits which accrued from the introduction of machine banking, the impact of the new technology was considerable and all-pervasive: the new machines had an obvious presence, which often required reconstruction of the office space needed to accommodate them; working them necessitated new work practices; and, their impact on social relations at work was significant and extensive. The extent of this influence, and the degree to which employees were aware that mechanisation impinged directly on their daily lives at work, is demonstrated by the multitude of articles and cartoons on the subject which appeared in the banks' staff magazines published between 1928 and 1935. Three cartoons will suffice to illustrate the conscious perceptions of bank workers. First, Figure 2.5 illustrates not only the radical transformation of the work process, with hand-written ledgers replaced by machine-processed records, but also aspects of gender associated with feminisation of the clerical labour force and the working environment.[66] Although this picture undoubtedly overromanticises the lost gentlemanly attitude to female clerks, clearly the implications of women workers becoming extensions of a machine was evident to all bank workers. Second, issues of control and supervision of a branch bank are raised in Figure 2.6. Here representatives from headquarter offices, senior staff employed in the Inspection Department, appear as technicians arriving to scrutinise and fine-tune operation of a mechanical banking system at the local level. Finally, there were the customers. In addition to their own trepidations concerning change at work, bank workers were well aware of public anxiety concerning mechanisation.[67] This apprehension was not confined to aspects of security nor to the accuracy of record-keeping. In Figure 2.7 an attempt to

Figure 2.8 Mechanised banking at the Leicester Branch of the Westminster Bank, *circa* 1938. (*NatWest Group Archives*)

defraud a branch with a forged cheque has shocking consequences – but the cartoon also carries the implication that impersonal service threatened to damage the personal relationship which so many customers valued highly. As these cartoons so clearly illustrate, recognition of the cost cutting aspects of bank mechanisation alone would represent a failure to appreciate the far-reaching impact of this managerial and technical transformation.

Conclusions

During the interwar period a managerial transformation of the 'Big Five' banks was achieved which belies their popular reputation as holders of conservative and traditionalistic attitudes. The solitary bank office or the small scale banking organisations which developed as the initial steps taken on the road to extensive branch banking were already regarded as quaint historic novelties by the Edwardian period. Banks as large business organisations with central offices overseeing numerous distant branches were already established before the First World War. While military service was an exogenous shock which altered temporarily the employment structure of the banks, some of whom admitted women as banking staff for the first time,[68] subsequent developments within the banks produced a discriminatory employment structure with selection by gender. The employment of women, at lower rates of remuneration, was not the only response of the banks to rising staff costs and machines were introduced in order to substitute capital for labour. However, the typical pattern was to jointly substitute female labour and accounting machines for male labour. Senior officers in the banks, having noted that female workers were adept in the use of keyboards and were employed in jobs which, by definition, excluded any promotion to managerial or executive positions, saw the potential offered by reorganization and mechanization to cut costs, standardize practices, impose supervision at all levels of activity, raise efficiency and, more generally, centralise the management of large scale, corporate organisations.

Although these developments have been documented in at least three of the more recent bank histories,[69] the extent of this change has largely eluded economic historians of the interwar period who, for the most part, while noting the amalgamation movement, do not recognise the extent and significance of the associated changes in management structure and organisation.[70] Alford provides a very recent example of a literature which presents senior British bank officials as insular, amateurish, elitist, resistant to change and generally conservative:

'Yet there is evidence to suggest that merchant banks and other financial institutions (including British multinational banks overseas) proved slow to adapt to changing conditions. Lack of entrepreneurial enterprise was no less evident in City banking parlours than it was in company boardrooms.'[71]

In fact, professional management had replaced entrepreneurial enterprise in the 'Big Five' by the end of the 1920s.

In similar vein, the role of the banks in the alleged slow adoption of the corporate form in Britain provides the central thesis of Cottrell's recent essay, 'Finance and the germination of the British corporate economy'. This outlines the bank amalgamation movement and the development of national branch banking but, beyond mention of 'management styles' and 'the introduction of mechanised book-keeping',[72] does not examine the emergence of corporate structures and the evolution of managerial organisation among the 'Big Five'. Rather, Cottrell opines that 'common to both large manufacturing companies and large commercial banks was the lack of managerial development, a corporate lag that was to persist until the 1960s'.[73]

This view is incompatible with the interwar managerial transformation of the 'Big Five'. Indeed, given the pace and extent of change between 1928 and 1934, similar changes in other business organisations might even warrant the description 'revolutionary' rather than 'evolutionary'. However, to affirm the extent of managerial changes within the 'Big Five' is not to suggest that all their managerial difficulties had been solved in the interwar period, nor that there was no potential for further development.

In addition, while it may be true of some elements of the manufacturing and extractive industries, for the banking sector, at least, there is also good reason to reject Alford's suggestion that the interwar years inherited a general reluctance to change the *status quo post bellum* which impeded the introduction of new techniques, methods and managerial structures:

'Central to the needs of business reorganization was technical change involving new labour practices and reduced manning levels. The war conspired to fuse the interests of businessmen and organized labour in their resistance to innovation.'[74]

In the banking sector significant managerial and institutional changes began before the First World War, continued in novel directions during the War, and resulted in new organisational arrangements afterwards. In the case of commercial banking, at least: Britain was not slow to start down the path to corporate structures; Britain was not tentative in its adoption of these techniques; and, Britain did not lag significantly behind the USA, or Germany. Moreover, although British bankers were willing to learn from the practices and experiences of their contemporaries abroad, their implementation of this process was carefully considered, indigenously determined, and not imitative in nature.

Furthermore, this thesis can be gauged against Chandler's summary of the three pronged strategy adopted by managers of the modern industrial enterprise:[75] from 1900, if not before, the senior officials of British commercial banks: first, did invest in production facilities large enough to exploit the potential economies of scale or scope of the relevant technology; second, did invest in a national and international marketing and distribution network, so that the volume of sales might keep pace with the new volume of production; and, third, did invest in management so to benefit fully from the investment made in production facilities and the marketing and distribution networks. For a 'Big Five' British bank, the first two of these inter-related criteria were both achieved by investment in an extensive branch network controlled by a central head office; this strategy was also permissive of the adoption of new technology which not only cut costs but also increased the potential for managerial co-ordination and supervision. Here, investment in human capital, Chandler's third criterion, was essential. In English commercial banks managers were recruited and trained to ensure that they were able to administer the enlarged facilities and increased personnel required for production and distribution on a much enlarged scale; in addition, at the strategic level of senior management, systems were developed to monitor and co-ordinate those two basic functional activities and to plan and allocate resources for future production and distribution.

Perhaps Chandler's analytical framework can be made general; maybe its range stretches beyond the manufacturing sector. Here it is used to investigate the nature of investment to secure capabilities by the commercial banks, which are representative of the services sectors and, specifically, the financial services. Given the nature of Britain's economic development, it is not surprising that this development was well-established in the services sectors from a very early point in the history of this global phenomenon. However, this suggestion does not seem so far removed from Chandler's original conception which stressed the initial development and impact of managerial achievements in the service sectors: first, by the railroad, urban transit and telegraph companies and, second, by the urban departmental stores which took advantage of the distributive opportunities provided by the former.[76] Yet another theme of Chandler's discussion of the emergence of the modern industrial corporation is the powerful competitive advantage achieved by a small number of first movers who quickly come to dominate their industry as oligopolists:[77] given their size, longevity and the structure of their industry, the 'Big Five' British banks provide not only an excellent example of 'first mover advantage' but also a manifestation of the limitations of this concept.[78]

The developments in managerial structures and practices related here also have implications for any appraisal of the role of the 'Big Five' in the British economy. It would appear that much of the criticism voiced about the performance of the commercial banks in the interwar period has been misdirected.[79] In the 1920s, they were, of course, engaged collectively in industrial finance to an extent which was unprecedented. Moreover, it was because of this involvement that the commercial banks became so enmeshed in the rationalisation schemes which recently have been documented by various economic historians.[80] However, it is also clear that the commercial banks were themselves very much alive to the potential benefits of new management structures and new technology; specifically, they assessed and implemented the then progressive information technology offered by machine accounting.

In making their assessments of this machinery, the banks benefited from information relating not only to existing users of these capital goods, ranging from insurance firms to railway companies, both at home and abroad, but also from the manufacturers of office machinery themselves, who sought custom by providing advice about management information systems.[81] By 1930 senior managers of the 'Big Five' were well aware of the potentialities and pitfalls of technical change and the introduction of new management systems – from their own experiences. This alone must have confirmed to them that, although advice came cheap (and criticism even cheaper), what was really important was to know the organisation of an individual business inside out. Moreover, by the mid-1930s, with the diffusion of budgetary control and the development of more accurate costing systems, the major clearing banks could look forward to clients providing better quality information, confident that senior bank staff would be sufficiently experienced and better equipped to express an expert opinion on the technical excellence, credit worthiness and potential profitability of an applicant's business.[82] However, although the 'Big Five' had made the transition to the corporate form by the early 1930s, they could only encourage by example and exhortation, leading where many other firms would eventually follow.

In the four decades before 1939 managerial structures of the 'Big Five' in Britain were transformed, albeit with different emphasises in each case and with responses which were determined by individual factors that had shaped the historical development of each bank's corporate culture. When we turn to the development of internal management structures, so essential for the elements which comprise the Corporate Economy, we find that British commercial banks had developed the structures which define competitive managerial capitalism. Furthermore, the managerial systems introduced before 1925 were the subject of subsequent systematic review. The introduction of new technology, in the form of machine accounting, was taken as an opportunity to assess not only the efficiency of the existing managerial systems but also to envisage alternatives – the banks engaged in a comprehensive review of their practices and systematically appraised options for the future.[83] Recognition of this managerial dynamic calls into question not only the assumption, voiced not infrequently by economic historians of the interwar period, that the banks were conservative and ineffective, but also assertions of their naive disinterest in corporate development in the industrial sector.

The last word, like the first, perhaps should go to Keynes who demonstrated in 1927 a particularly percipient view of the future of banking organisation and mechanisation. In response to a question about the Labour Party's policy on nationalisation he reiterated his view that the 'Big Five' were already semi-socialised, or nationalised; in addition to their activities being of national scope, there was already a divorce between ownership and management and the banks were largely controlled by those in the receipt of salaries. Furthermore, indicating his appreciation of the extent, role and potential of the corporate organisation in the corporate economy, and anticipating correctly the reformist nature of twentieth century Labour governments, Keynes continued:

"'The banks are evolving most of the things the Labour party wants everything to be like". What the Labour party wants is to make all other businesses like banks.'[84]

Acknowledgments

My thanks to the Nuffield Foundation which financed this research [Research Grant SOC/100 (1401)] and to the archivists who offered their hospitality and advice concerning the records which record the history of the 'Big Five' British Banks: Jessie Campbell (Barclays Bank Group Archives); Edwin Green (HSBC Group Archives); Dr John Booker (Lloyds Bank Archives); and, Fiona McColl, Susan Snell and Derek Hammond (NatWest Group Archives). Professor Leslie Hannah provided much appreciated encouragement and assistance though he, like all mentioned here, is not responsible for the content. Dr Duncan Ross deserves a mention for 'leaning' on me to ensure that a version of this paper was scrutinised at the Monetary History Group Meeting in November 1997; I also benefited from the constructively critical response of economic historians at the University of Leeds. A version of this paper was kindly presented on my behalf by Professor Michael Collins to the 'Banks as Firms' session of the 1998 International Economic History Conference; Dr Trevor Boyns, Professor Geoffrey Channon and Professor Ranald Michie generously provided valuable suggestions incorporated here.

Notes

1 C. H. Lee, *The British economy since 1700: a macroeconomic perspective* (Cambridge 1986); Z. Griliches (ed.), *Output measurement in the services sectors* (Chicago 1992); A. J. Field, 'The relative productivity of American distribution, 1869–1992', *Research in Economic History*, vol. 16 (1996), pp. 1–37.

2 N. Gemmell and P. Wardley, 'The contribution of services to British economic growth, 1856–1913', *Explorations in Economic History*, vol. 27 (1991), pp. 299–321.

3 C. H. Lee, 'Economic growth, structural change, labour productivity and industrialisation, 1860–1913', research paper, University of Aberdeen (1986); C. H. Lee, 'Kaldor's laws and economic growth in historical perspective: the industrial economies 1880–1973', research paper, University of Aberdeen (1987); S. N. Broadberry, 'Anglo-German productivity differences 1870–1990: a sectoral analysis', *European Review of Economic History*, vol. 1 (1997), pp. 247–267; S. N. Broadberry, 'Forging ahead, falling behind and catching-up: a sectoral analysis of Anglo-American productivity differences, 1870–1990', *Research in Economic History*, vol. 17 (1997), pp. 1–37.

4 P. Wardley, 'The anatomy of big business: aspects of corporate development in the twentieth century', *Business History*, vol. 33, no. 2 (1991), pp. 268–296.

5 R. Levine, 'Financial development and economic growth: views and agenda', *Journal of Economic Literature*, vol. XXXV (1997), p. 688.

6 Walter Bagehot, Joseph Schumpeter, John Hicks, Alexander Gerschenkron and Raymond Goldsmith appear as Levine's proponents of the importance of the financial system and its institutions; the dissenters, a smaller brethren, include Robert Lucas, Anand Chandavarkar and Joan Robinson; Levine, 'Financial development', p. 688.

60   Peter Wardley

7   M. Collins, 'English bank development within a European context', *Economic History Review*, vol. LI, no. 1 (1998), pp. 1–24.
8   A. D. Chandler, Jnr., *Strategy and Structure: chapters in the history of industrial enterprise* (Cambridge, Mass. 1962); A. D. Chandler, Jnr., *The Visible Hand: the managerial revolution in American business* (Cambridge, Mass. 1977); L. Hannah, *The rise of the corporate economy* (London 1973).
9   P. L. Payne, 'The emergence of the large scale company in Great Britain, 1870–1914', *Economic History Review*, vol. 20 (1967), pp. 519–542.
10 A. D. Chandler, Jnr., *Scale and Scope: the dynamics of industrial capitalism* (Cambridge, Mass., 1990), p. 12.
11 Chandler, *Scale and Scope*, p. 8.
12 L. Hannah, 'Scale and Scope: towards a European Visible Hand?', *Business History*, vol. 33, no. 2 (1991), pp. 297–309; B. Supple, 'Scale and Scope: Alfred Chandler and the dynamics of industrial capitalism', *Economic History Review*, vol. xliv, no. 3 (1991), pp. 500–514.
13 A different view of industrial development in the United States which stresses speciality production and regional networks is provided by P. Scranton, *Endless Novelty: Speciality Production and American Industrialization* (Princeton, N. J., 1997).
14 Y. Cassis, *Big Business: the European experience in the twentieth century* (Oxford 1997).
15 For example, W. Lazonick, *Business organization and the myth of the market economy* (New York 1991), p. 48–49.
16 P. Wardley, 'The anatomy of big business: aspects of corporate development in the twentieth century', *Business History*, vol. 33, no. 2 (1991), pp. 268–296; C. Schmitz, *The growth of big business in the United States and Western Europe, 1850–1939* (London 1993); L. Hannah, 'Symposium on "The American Miracle": Afterthoughts', *Business and Economic History*, vol. 24, no. 2 (1995), pp. 246–262; P. Wardley, 'The emergence of Big Business: the largest corporate employers of labour in the United Kingdom, Germany and the United States c. 1907.' *Business History*, vol. 41, no. 4 (1999), pp. 88–116.
17 Wardley, 'Anatomy', p. 288. One of the indicators most favoured by proponents of the thesis of British entrepreneurial failure in this period, the inability of British businessmen to develop large corporations, thereby fails this most obvious test.
18 M. Collins, *Banks and industrial finance in Britain 1800–1939* (London 1991); F. Capie and M. Collins, 'Deficient suppliers? Commercial banks in the United Kingdom, 1870–1980' and D. M. Ross, 'The 'Macmillan gap' and the British credit market in the 1930s': both in P. L. Cottrell, A. Teichova and T. Yuzawa (eds.), *Finance in the age of the corporate economy* (Aldershot 1997), pp. 164–183, pp. 209–226.
19 M. Best and J. Humphries, 'The City and industrial decline' in B. Elbaum and W. Lazonick (eds.), *The decline of the British economy* (London 1986), pp. 223–239; S. Tolliday, *Business, Banking and Politics: the case of British steel, 1918–1936* (Cambridge 1987).
20 D. Ross, 'Information, collateral and British bank lending in the 1930s' in Y. Cassis, G. Feldman, and U. Olsson (eds.), *The evolution of financial institutions and market in twentieth century Europe* (Aldershot 1995), pp. 273–294.

21 *(Macmillan) Committee on Finance & Industry Report* (London 1931), especially pp. 102–105, 161–173 and the dissenting views attached to the Report, pp. 190–281.

22 The first three indicators listed here receive fuller attention here, though data for the other three are readily available (for example, deposits and advances were recorded in monthly returns of the London clearing banks and reported profits were published in the balance sheets).

23 A. R. Holmes and E. Green, *Midland: 150 years of banking business* (London 1986), pp. 332–335, provides actual profits for the Midland Bank; comparative data for Barclays Bank have been estimated by Leslie Hannah (forthcoming).

24 See also M. Collins, 'The growth of the firm in the domestic banking sector', in M. W. Kirby and M. B. Rose (eds.), *Business enterprise in modern Britain: from the eighteenth to the twentieth century* (London 1994), pp. 278–286.

25 F. Capie, 'Structure and Performance in British Banking, 1870–1939', in P. L. Cottrell and D. E. Moggridge, *Money and Power: essays in honour of L. S. Pressnell* (London 1988), pp. 73–102; P. L. Cottrell, 'Finance and the germination of the British corporate economy', and C. Munn, 'Banking on branches: the origins and development of branch banking in the United Kingdom'; both in Cottrell, Teichova, and Yuzawa, *Finance*, pp. 5–36 and 37–51 respectively.

26 F. Capie and G. Rodrik-Bali, 'Concentration in British Banking 1880–1920', *Business History*, 24 (1982), pp. 280–292.

27 For contemporaries the term 'rationalisation' was often loosely applied to any kind of managerial change, including: amalgamation; merger; reorganisation; the adoption of new technology, often American in origin; measures taken to increase concentration or even reduce the range of product lines. In the case of the 'Big Five' rationalisation does appear to have been pursued in the narrower, economic sense: that is, the managed redeployment of capital and labour to achieve optimal, or near optimal, output and productivity after a rational assessment of the market and available factors of production. For example, between 1920 and 1929 the Midland Bank established 638 new branches but also closed 91 branches to curtail duplication of local banking provision following amalgamations with the Metropolitan Bank (1914) and the London Joint Stock Bank (1918), Holmes and Green, *Midland*, pp. 127, 131, 169–170; see also J. R. Winton, *Lloyds Bank 1918–1969* (London, 1982), p. 70. Evidence of 'Rationalisation' has been suggested as a test of Chandler's assertion that the conventional ideas associated with personal capitalism dominated in interwar Britain by J. Wilson, *British business history, 1720–1994* (London 1995), p. 144.

28 Holmes and Green, *Midland*, p. 175; Winton, *Lloyds Bank 1918–1969*, p. 51.

29 At the beginning of the interwar period it was commonly held to be the largest bank in the world.

30 A. W. Tuke and R. J. H. Gillman, *Barclays Bank Limited 1926–1969: some recollections* (London 1972), p. 21–23; Holmes and Green, *Midland*, pp. 167, 196.

31 Tuke and Gillman, *Barclays Bank Limited 1926–1969*, pp. 20–23; F. Carnevali,'Finance in the regions: the case of England after 1945' in Cassis, Feldman, and Olsson (eds.), *The evolution of financial institutions*, pp. 295–314.

32 W. F. Crick and J. E. Wadsworth, *A hundred years of joint stock banking* (London 1958), p. 341.

33 Crick and Wadsworth, *A hundred years*, p. 340–341.

34 For example, see Holmes and Green, *Midland*: p. 110, figure 4.1, 'The Midland board and management structure, c. 1900'; and p. 191, figure 7.1, 'Midland Bank board and management structure, c. 1929'.

35 L. le M. Minty, *English banking methods* (London 1930).

36 Minty, *English banking methods*, p. 127–129.

37 By the author.

38 Winton, *Lloyds Bank*, p. 34.

39 Holmes and Green, *Midland*, p. 132.

40 Tuke and Gillman, *Barclays Bank Limited*, p. 81.

41 Like Figure 1, Figure 2 is a "model" or archetype and derives from Minty, *English Banking Methods*, pp. 129, 445–532.

42 Minty, *English banking methods*, pp. 127–129.

43 Minty, *English banking methods*, pp. 129–140.

44 The origins, nature and development of *The Bible*, the alphabetical listing of employees of Lloyds Bank, are described in K. Stovel, M. Savage and P. Bearman, 'Ascription into achievement: models of career systems at Lloyds Bank, 1890–1970', *American Journal of Sociology*, vol. 102, no 2 (1996), pp. 366–376.

45 P. B. Doeringer and M. J. Piore, *Internal labour markets and manpower analysis* (Lexington, Mass. 1971).

46 Bank managers were one of a few high status groups who could vouch for an individual applying for a British passport.

47 Women also experienced other forms of discrimination relating to remuneration: those re-employed in 1920 often received no recognition of their previous employment and admission of women to the banks' contributory pension schemes was delayed. At Lloyds Bank, for example, the contributory pension scheme was introduced for men in 1930 and for women in 1936; Winton, *Lloyds Bank*, p. 74.

48 Women staff were expected to be single and to resign on marriage; this was not solely a gender issue as junior male staff were strongly encouraged to remain bachelors in the early years of their career.

49 O. E. Williamson, M. L. Wachter and J. E. Harris, 'Understanding the employment relation: the analysis of idiosyncratic exchange', *Bell Journal of Economics and Management Science*, 6 (1975), pp. 250–278.

50 J. T. Addison and W. S. Siebert, *The market for labor: an analytical treatment* (Santa Monica, California 1979), p. 188.

51 Office technology and its early twentieth century usage is extensively illustrated and described in D. Gardey, 'Pour une histoire technique du métier dee comptable: évolution des conditions practiques du travail de comptabilité du début du XIX siècle à la veille de la Seconde guerre mondiale', *Troisiemes journées d'Histoire de la Comptabilité: Hommes, saviors et practiques de la Comptabilité* (Nantes, 1997), pp. 3–36.

52 S. J. Gould, 'Cordelia's dilemma', *Dinosaur in a haystack* (London 1996), pp. 123–132.

53 H. C. F Holgate, 'The scope for further mechanization', *The Banker*, vol. xliii (1938), pp. 56–57.

54 Anon., 'Mechanical accounting', *The Banker*, vol. xi (1929), pp. 164–165.

55 H. L. Rouse, 'The progress of mechanization', *The Banker*, vol. xvi (1930), p. 125.

56 H. L. Rouse, 'A general review of six years of mechanization', *The Banker*, vol. xxvii (1933), p. 238.

57 The adoption of this term by the Midland Bank may have had unanticipated consequences in the historical analysis of twentieth century British banking: the use of 'centralisation' to describe grouping by branch for information processing purposes seems to have contributed to the perception that the Midland Bank was more 'centralised' than its rivals.

58 Minty, *English banking methods*, pp. 192–195.

59 Rouse, 'The progress of mechanization', pp. 122–126.

60 A. C. Parker, 'Machine accountancy at Westminster Bank, Lothbury', *The Banker*, vol. xxvii (July 1933), p. 61.

61 Parker, 'Machine accountancy', pp. 64–65.

62 Parker, 'Machine accountancy', p. 66.

63 Parker, 'Machine accountancy', p. 60.

64 Rouse, 'A general review', p. 244.

65 This is an estimate of annual salary savings, minus machine costs, including depreciation, at the 'Big Five' Banks in 1939. Based on information contained in contemporary sources, including articles cited here and numerous internal reports concerning mechanization, it is a smaller saving than that suggested either by *ex ante* predictions or by savings reported by the staff closely associated with mechanisation. Further details will be provided in a forthcoming analysis of output, employment and productivity in the British banking industry.

66 For the United States, an extensive discussion of gender, the development of clerical occupations and the construction of work in commercial offices is provided by A. Kwolek-Folland, *Engendering Business: Men and Women in the Corporate Office, 1870–1930* (Baltimore 1995).

67 'A Banker', 'Bank Mechanization as affecting Personnel and Public', *The Banker*, vol. xliii (1938), pp. 60–61.

68 E. R. Long, 'The future position of women clerks in banks', *Journal of the Institute of Banking*, vol. XLIV (1923), pp. 114–23.

69 Holmes and Green, *Midland*, pp. 171–174, 190–193; Tuke and Gillman, *Barclays*, pp. 93–94; and, Winton, *Lloyds Bank*, p. 84–91.

70 For example, S. Pollard, *The development of the British economy 1914–1980* (3rd edn, London, 1983), p. 147: 'The joint-stock banks had, by the early 1930s, fully completed the process of amalgamation that was all but consummated by 1920.'

71 B. W. E. Alford, *Britain in the World Economy since 1880* (London 1996), p. 121.

72 P. L. Cottrell, 'Finance and the germination of the British corporate economy', p. 26.

73 As further evidence of corporate lag, Cottrell also suggests that few direct communications existed between the large banks and the large manufacturing firms, Cottrell, 'Finance', p. 31. However, by the 1930s a dense and complex network of inter-locking directorates had developed to link the boards of Britain's largest companies which encompassed the 'Big Five' Banks: P.

Wardley, 'Aspects of Corporate Development in the Twentieth Century: the Anatomy of Britain's Largest Fifty Companies in 1904, 1934 and 1985 by Absolute Size, Relative Size, Concentration, Geographical Location and Inter-Locking Directorates', UWE Research Paper in Business History, no. 1 (1990); also see the author's 'Big Business' webpages at the University of the West of England's website: www.uwe.ac.uk.

74 Alford, *Britain*, p. 126.

75 Chandler, *Scale and Scope*, p. 8; cited at p. 73 above.

76 Chandler, *Strategy and Structure*, p. 232; Field, 'The relative productivity', p. 18–19.

77 Chandler, *Scale and Scope*, p. 8

78 The Midland Bank survived until 1992, when it was acquired by the Hong Kong and Shanghai Bank to form HSBC Holdings plc. The National Westminster Bank, created by the merger of the Provincial Bank and the Westminster Bank in 1970, survived until 2000 when, as the NatWest Group, it was acquired by the Royal Bank of Scotland. At the beginning of the twenty first century, therefore, only two of the 'Big Five' survived as independent banking corporations: Barclays Bank and Lloyds Bank.

79 F. Capie and M. Collins 'Deficient suppliers?' pp. 169–176.

80 S. Tolliday, *Business, Banking and Politics*, p. 177; M. Kirby, 'The Lancashire cotton industry in the interwar years: a study in organisational change', *Business History*, vol. 16. (1974), pp. 144–159.

81 An excellent example of this interaction is provided by JoAnne Yates, 'Co-evolution of Information-processing technology and use: interaction between Life Insurance and Tabulating industries', *Business History Review*, vol. 67 (Spring 1993), pp. 1–51.

82 C. R. Curtis, 'Office rationalisation and the banks', *The Banker*, vol. xxxv (July 1935), pp. 49–54.

83 Recent research has provided similar examples of management reorganisation introduced to achieve administrative and financial control during the interwar period. For example, L. Cailluet, 'Accounting and accountants as essential elements in the development of central administration during the interwar period: management ideology and technology at Alais, Froges et Camargue (AFC-Pechiney)', *Accounting, Business and Financial History*, vol. 7, no. 3 (1997), pp. 295–314 provides an excellent example of a large French industrial corporation which transformed its managerial structures and procedures, incorporating office machinery worked largely by females, to cope with the challenges of increased scale, scope and geographic diversification.

84 Anon., 'Mr J. M. Keynes on banking services', *Journal of the Institute of Banking*, vol. xlviii (November 1927), p. 497.

Retrospect and postscript

Before the publication of this article British banks tended to be taken for granted, if not slighted, by economic historians, and almost ignored by business historians, unless their research was focused upon the history of a specific bank. This article challenged widely held assumptions that in the interwar years British banks lagged behind their counterparts in the more developed economies and that their senior managers were old-fashioned and conservative in their business practices. My article demonstrated that senior managers in British banks were very well-informed about contemporary developments in management thought and methods and were well able to act decisively and quickly to implement radical change; this was a story about the management of institution-wide complex change rather than just the simple introduction of mechanical devices to aid the recording of financial transactions.

The process of bank mechanisation was a closely directed and multi-faceted transformation that saw not only the introduction of new technology but also associated major changes that included: the standardisation of data transfer between the head office of a bank and its branches; the re-organisation of labour processes, with its associated gender consequences for bank clerks (commercial considerations prevailed here: it was the cost-benefit analysis associated with bank mechanisation in the 1920s, rather than imperatives of the Great War, that motivated the permanent employment of large numbers of female bank employees [Wardley, 2011]); and, through a variety of media, including staff magazines and newspaper articles, the development of a new self-conscious 'modern' corporate culture (this was a culture that embraced all 'stake-holders': shareholders and customers as well as employees at all levels with the banks). Clearly, the major commercial banks were transformed during the interwar years; however, given that this occurred at a time when 'rationalisation' was a popular topic, albeit that there was much disagreement about its definition, it must be stressed that in many ways the banks were pioneers and at the forefront of developments.

Serendipity played a part in the publication of this article. At its launch the *Journal of Industrial History* filled a unique niche in academic publishing. Not only did it aspire to encompass a range of approaches to the study of industrial phenomena, thus encouraging historiographical debate, but its high publication standards offered its authors the possibility to employ a variety of high-quality visual aids, including tables, diagrams, graphs, maps and photographs. Hitherto, the journals that served business history in Britain had been heavily loaded with text and very light on visual aids (in the USA the journal *Enterprise and Society* had recently presented a similar challenge to the traditional publishing format). My article depended in large part on its visual aids to bolster its revisionist case; for example, the cartoons faithfully reproduced from the banks' staff magazines dramatically captured the nature and perceptions of mechanisation at the branches and at head office.

The editors of the *Journal of Industrial History* had also welcomed the use of theory; this appeared here in the form of an explicit, but non-mathematical, statement that senior bank managers, like those of other capitalist corporations, had stated economic objectives and took rational decisions on the basis of the information available to them; this assertion was supported by quantitative evidence relating to both mechanisation and rationalisation.

Another serendipitous factor was the dawning of an awareness among economic historians and business historians of the significance, and soon to be predominance, of the services sectors. I have little doubt that at its conception the *Journal of Industrial History* was expected to be a vehicle for historical investigations of manufacturing activity, rather than a venue for the academic investigation of 'industries', as indicated by labelling descriptors such as the 'brewing industry' or 'automobile industry'. Here, again, the editors were generous and welcomed a study that clearly focused on a service sector activity, the *banking industry*.

Finally, one indicator of the success of an article, or otherwise, can be assessed by its reception by scholars in the relevant academic discipline. Given its rapid adoption in the literatures of economic history and business history, and the lack of a proposed case to the contrary, the revisionist case made in this article appears to have become the new orthodoxy. It has informed more positive assessments of the contribution of the services sectors in British economic development; for example, the *Cambridge Economic History of Modern Britain* (Floud and Johnson, 2004). Similarly, it contributed to the generally optimistic assessment of the

British financial sector in the twentieth century presented by Stephen Broadberry's *Market Services and the Productivity Race 1850–2000: British Performance in the International Perspective*.

However, while every citation, like all publicity, might be welcomed by an author, not all citations are accurate. For example, given the systemic changes wrought in the interwar British banking industry that are documented in this article, I was surprised to find it cited by Bernardo Bátiz-Lazo and Douglas Wood (2002) to support a taxonomy and timeline which dates to the developments from 1945 to 1965 in the banking industry which had been introduced successfully in the 1920s.

I have two retrospective thoughts. First, the world economy experienced a major downturn within eight years of the publication of this article. This economic depression has been attributed to many causes and one of the more popular contemporary explanations highlighted the burgeoning use of information technology (IT) in the previous decade which had automated financial transactions and underpinned business systems. By contrast, in the 1930s, commentators had not suggested that the recently introduced technology associated with mechanised banking was a causal factor contributing to, let alone the major cause of, the interwar Great Depression. Here there is scope for a story that provides an international comparison; this would highlight the use of machine banking in systems characterised by branched banking, these included all the world's richer nations except in the United States of America (where unit banks used banking machinery, but differently). It also appears likely to me that, relative to the interwar experience, in the decade after 2000 senior bank staff had much less understanding of either the technology they had adopted or the processes delivered by the IT at their disposal. In the British case, the quality of the staff appraisals made in the interwar period, both in terms of the assessors and those assessed, can be seen in the significance of junior staff who had been tasked to implement machine banking who became senior managers after World War Two.

Finally, there was at least one aspect of this story that at the time of writing I failed to recognise. I took for granted on the part of my readers historical knowledge of the technological developments that had transformed the computing industry in the two decades before 2000. I should have stressed the continuity of IT developments throughout the twentieth century – one notable example being the persistence of the format of the Hollerith punch card as embodied by the evolution of the visual display screen (VDU). As a consequence, I may have given the impression that post–World War Two developments were more stark and more radical than was the case. In failing to emphasise this continuity I may have inadvertently made less obvious the evolutionary story which should dominate any interpretation of the adoption, diffusion and use of technology in the banking industry.

References

Bátiz-Lazo, Bernardo and Douglas Wood (2002) 'An Historical Appraisal of Information Technology in Commercial Banking', *Electronic Markets*, 12, 3, pp. 192–205.

Broadberry, Stephen (2004) *Market Services and the Productivity Race 1850–2000: British Performance in the International Perspective*. Cambridge: Cambridge University Press.

Floud, Roderick and Paul Johnson (eds.) (2004) *The Cambridge Economic History of Modern Britain*. Cambridge: Cambridge University Press.

Wardley, Peter (2011) 'Women, Mechanization and Cost Savings in Twentieth Century British Banks and Other Financial Institutions', in M. Richardson and P. Nicholls (eds.), *A Business and Labour History of Britain*, pp. 32–59. Houndsmill: Palgrave Macmillan.

Chapter 3

Did they have it so good? Small firms and British monetary policy in the 1950s*

Francesca Carnevali

The Fifties were years of economic and social progress for Britain: by 1950, pre-war levels of consumption had been restored and over the following ten years the economy grew as never before. Economic prosperity was made tangible by the virtual disappearance of unemployment and earnings rose faster than prices, allowing increased mass consumption of luxuries such as cars, white goods and holidays, while home-ownership doubled.[1] Such clearly perceivable improvements in the standard of living meant that most people would have agreed with the new Prime Minister, Harold Macmillan, when, in his famous speech of June 1957, he said, 'most of our people have never had it so good. Go around the country, go to the industrial towns, go to the farms, and you will see a state of prosperity such as we have never had in my lifetime – not indeed ever in the history of this country'.

Much less perceivable at the time was the backdrop to this picture of prosperity; the recurring balance of payments crises and the spectre of inflation, both of which threatened the stability of the pound, and consequently Britain's international position.

Monetary policy was one of the main tools used by successive Conservative Chancellors to manage consumer demand, in the attempt to maintain full employment while controlling the balance of payments and defending the value of the pound in the 'running up' to the achievement of full convertibility. Government policy to manage the growth of aggregate demand included raising the Bank Rate, the imposition of controls on hire-purchase and on the Capital Issues Committee, and exercising pressure on the banks to restrain their lending. British policy makers at the time did not understand that under a pegged exchange rate system where Britain was not the reserve centre, direct controls could not affect aggregate monetary conditions. In fact, it was the country's external position, vis-à-vis its Bretton Woods peg, that determined whether monetary policy had to be tightened or could be relaxed.[2]

Even though the policy framework in which the macro-economy operated was not understood by the government, it is important to assess the impact these policies had on British industry;[3] this paper addresses this issue by focusing on the restrictions on bank lending and their effect on small manufacturing firms' capacity for expansion. The main contention of this paper is that while all firms, regardless of size, saw their activities curtailed by monetary policy, small firms bore the brunt of the credit restrictions as, unlike large companies, they had no other source of finance beyond their banks. The paper shows how for a number of firms the adoption of new machinery was conditional on their ability to raise money from their banks since overdraft facilities, though nominally not used for capital purposes, could release resources for the purchase of machinery or the expansion of premises.[4]

The credit restrictions exacerbated an existing gap in the provision of finance for small firms, known as the Macmillan Gap,[5] as firms saw their overdrafts reduced or curtailed. The firms' response to the credit restrictions – the strategy they adopted to satisfy their need for capital – was to seek alternative, though costly, sources of funds such as hire purchase on plant and machinery. While contemporary commentators have analysed the uses of hire purchase during the 1950s, these studies have tended to concentrate on hire purchase for consumer credit. A detailed analysis of the scale and character of hire purchase for industrial purposes has largely been neglected in the historical study of financial institutions in the post-war period and this paper aims to redress the balance.[6]

Due to the lack of business archives and corporate histories, small firms belong to that 'voiceless majority' often neglected by historical analysis. The lack of archival evidence generated directly by a large enough number of small firms makes assessing the impact of government policies on this category of firms arduous. That is why, in the main, small firms have been left out of the debate on the micro-economic implications of 'stop-go'. Nevertheless 'voicelessness' in archival terms did not mean silence, in terms of small firms' own agency at the time. During the 1950s, the representatives of small firms, such as trade associations and chambers of commerce, remonstrated strongly against the government's monetary policy. The sessions of the 1959 Committee on the workings of the monetary system (also known as the Radcliffe Committee) became one of the main fora for these complaints. The memoranda of evidence and the minutes of the Committee provide previously unstudied qualitative and quantitative evidence, which offers a valuable insight into the difficulties faced by small firms at the time. The other source used for this paper is the survey conducted in 1956 by the Oxford

University Institute of Statistics for the purpose of establishing the financial difficulties of small manufacturing firms.[7] The data in the survey cover the first half of the 1950s, while the Radcliffe Committee details the second half. Material from the archives of the Bank of England has also been used to establish the reaction of the commercial banks to the credit restrictions. Finally, Board of Trade and Census of Distribution figures have been used to estimate the amount of hire purchase finance used by small firms at the time.

1. Small firms and the British economy

At the end of the 1960s, the Parliamentary Committee of Inquiry on Small Firms (hereafter, the Bolton Committee) ascertained that the British economy suffered from a long term decline in the number of small firms and in their contribution to output and employment. More significantly, the Committee's report revealed that while this decline was being experienced by all the developed countries, the process had gone further in Britain than elsewhere.[8] The implications of these findings in terms of Britain's industrial competitiveness are spelled out in a study on small firms and technological innovation, commissioned by the Committee and carried out by the University of Sussex. The study found that small firms accounted for approximately 10 per cent of the important innovations selected for the investigation over the period 1945–70. Their share of innovation was half of their share of employment and output, but more than twice their share of research and development expenditure, suggesting that the innovative *efficiency* of small firms was greater than that of large firms.[9] While in no way suggesting that all small firms were sources of technological change, the Committee argued that, because of the impossibility of selecting 'winners', the decline in the total number of small firms had important implications for the stock of potential innovations, and therefore for economic performance.

This paper, by concentrating on the external constraints experienced by small firms, does not want to suggest that there are no internal problems that can hinder their growth, such as managerial limitations, for example. However, as Edith Penrose argues so convincingly, a growing economy possesses 'interstices' left open by the expansion of larger firms, as their growth opens up new opportunities for investment. It is the struggle between small firms to occupy these spaces that tends to induce innovation in the process of production and in the variety of products.[10] Innovation in small firms takes the shape of a cumulative process and is determined crucially by the firm's liquidity at the moment

of the decision to change either process or product. Liquidity will determine the extension and the articulation of the first steps towards change.
Moreover, any uncertainty regarding the future availability of funds will
condition the firm's willingness to risk change.[11] Despite the Conservative government embracing a 'modernising' agenda in the 1960s,[12] it is
unlikely that in the 1950s the relevance of small firms was perceived as
going beyond their contribution to output and employment. Nevertheless, the innovative potential of small firms justifies establishing whether
the environment in which they found themselves in the post-war years
allowed them to develop this potential.[13]

2. Banking with brakes on

The goal of 'maintaining a high and stable level of employment after
the war' had to be achieved, together with price stability and budgetary stimuli, were used in the belief that these would control aggregate
demand.[14] As a consequence, the 1950s economy was characterised by
cycles of expansion followed by deflation in which policies dictated by
the government were used to counteract balance of payments crises or
changes in the level of unemployment. These 'stop-go' cycles, as they
have commonly been called, can be described by charting the macroeconomic policies that occurred year on year, and the following pages
analyse monetary policy focusing on the credit restrictions.

The Bank of England Act of 1946 limited the independence of the
clearing banks by stating that the Bank, if authorised by the Treasury,
could issue directives on how credit was to be allocated and eventually restricted, as deemed necessary in the public interest. This power
was never formally used and under the Labour Government bank lending increased relatively rapidly: by mid-1951 advances to all categories of customers had doubled since the end of the war. In 1951, the
rise of advances was further affected by inflation and by the build-up
of stocks caused by the outbreak of the Korean War. In April of that
year, Gaitskell, then Chancellor, felt compelled to ask the banks 'to
maintain a restraint in their credit policy',[15] thus showing his funda-
mental misunderstanding of the direction of causality in a pegged rate
system and of the policy framework in which he was operating. The
Chancellor left it to the banks to decide the day-by-day selection and
discrimination of lending, but he let it be known that the banks were
to favour projects concerning exports, agricultural development, trans-
port and the production of raw materials, and not to approve lending for
speculation or over-capitalisation. In November 1951, after numerous

meetings with the Governor of the Bank of England, the banks agreed to be firmer about advances to 'less essential industries', but in return requested an increase in the Bank Rate.[16] By the end of 1952, bank lending had fallen by 14% in real terms.[17] Although the officials at the Bank of England considered monetary policy to be working and regarded the fall in advances as 'encouraging', in the main the boards of the London Clearing Banks were sceptical of Treasury policies.[18] For instance, the Midland Bank knew that advances were falling because of reductions in stocks and prices, and that those firms that could were switching to public issues to finance their activities. The brunt of the restrictions was being felt by the smaller and more vulnerable borrowers, namely, those in the 'Personal and Professional' category. The chief general managers of Barclays, Lloyds and Westminster agreed that the fall in advances was not the Treasury's doing, but was due to foreign competition, and in the words of Edrington, Midland's chief general manager, 'things will be worse before they become better'.[19]

This restrictive phase was followed by a more expansionary orientation of policy within the 1953 budget, easing the pressure on banks, and reducing Bank rate. By 1955, the expansion of the economy had become a boom, drawing in an increasing amount of imports and pushing the balance of payments back into deficit, while prices and wages kept rising. Despite Butler's belief in the power of monetary measures,[20] such as the increase in bank rate to 4.5% in February and the re-introduction of hire-purchase restrictions, bank advances continued to increase. In July, the Treasury had to ask the banks to achieve a 'positive and significant reduction' in lending, but how the banks were to achieve this was left up to them.[21] In a meeting of the Committee of London Clearing Banks, it was decided that the banks would reduce advances by limiting the number of new applications accepted, by decreasing existing limits and by restricting the availability of finance to hire purchase companies and to customers in the 'Personal and Professional' category. The aim was to reduce advances by a total of 10% by December and memoranda were sent to branch managers with detailed instructions on how to deter customers.[22] By August, advances had declined in the 'Food', 'Retail', 'Other Financial', 'Personal and Professional', 'Other textiles' and 'Nationalised Industries' categories,[23] as customers kept away from the banks as they felt that 'it [was] no use asking'.[24]

Despite a further rise in Bank rate in February 1956 to 5.5%, the Treasury repeated its requests to the banks to maintain their restrictions on advances. Bank rate was lowered a year later to 5%, only to be increased to a 'crisis rate' of 7% in September, following the foreign exchange crisis.[25] Calls for a reduction in advances continued over these years, with the Chancellor (Macmillan first and Thorneycroft after him) taking the unprecedented step of regularly summoning the representatives of the commercial banks, instead of dealing with them through the Bank of England, to remind them of the seriousness of the government's policy.[26] Between 1955 and 1958 advances fell by a further 13% in real terms, until a rise in unemployment prompted the government to relax all controls in September 1958 and let the economy expand again.

As bank lending is not classified on the basis of the size of the borrower's business, it is not possible to determine exactly the fluctuations in lending to small firms. It is possible, however, to proxy this by using the figures for advances to the 'Personal and Professional' category of borrower as this group included advances to cover 'the provision of working capital for professional purposes, such as the purchase of machinery for a small manufacturer'.[27] In real terms, between 1951 and 1958 advances to this group of borrowers fell by 40 per cent, while advances as a whole fell by 18 per cent.[28] Reducing advances to smaller customers was much easier than denying credit to larger, corporate businesses, as the chairman of Lloyds, Sir Oliver Franks, candidly admitted.[29] The banks had to bear in mind that the Treasury gave preference to sectors involved in exports, at a time when the forty largest companies produced as much as 30% of all exports, while small firms only contributed directly to a quarter.

The continuation of the credit squeeze led to recurring questions regarding the impact of this measure on small firms. The representatives of the banks, in their meetings with the Governor of the Bank of England, reported the occurrence of a number of failures amongst the smaller concerns, though this did not trouble them unduly, as the level of bad debt was still very low.[30] Memos were circulated internally to the Bank, showing the increasing figures for bankruptcies, and by the end of 1956 the Bank was well aware that the credit squeeze was having an adverse effect on small firms.[31] Nevertheless, there is no mention in the Bank of England's files of possible measures that could be taken to avoid the credit restrictions from forcing small firms into liquidation.[32]

The absence of concern about the impact of policy on the real economy is well documented by the following episode. In July 1955, the MP for Wednesbury (a Black Country constituency) lamented the effect the credit restrictions were having on small firms in his constituency. He defined the Black Country as the 'stronghold of family business'; within ten miles of Wednesbury Town Hall there were no fewer than 10,000 small manufacturing concerns, each employing less than fifty people.

Most of these firms worked as subcontractors to the car industry and the MP feared that since these firms were not *directly* involved in exports they would suffer badly from the restrictions.[33] In his view, a reduction in credit would affect the small manufacturers very seriously since 'the people running these small family concerns have always been taught to look to the banks for money with which to modernise and expand their business. They know nothing of the money market'. The MP addressed Parliament to ask the government to impose on the banks some sort of regulation, which would prevent them from reducing advances at the expense of smaller customers. He was answered by the Economic Secretary to the Treasury, Sir Edward Boyle, in terms that leave little doubt that the fate of small firms was not one of the major concerns of the Treasury in formulating policies to curtail demand and maintain low inflation. One of the Treasury's aims was 'to encourage firms to postpone their marginal investment plans and, whenever possible, to postpone replacing their fixed assets'. Credit restrictions were to accomplish this and, in the words of Sir Edward, the Government '[were] right to attempt to reduce internal pressure by asking the banks themselves to take what steps they regard[ed] as necessary to reduce the volume of credit'. The smaller businesses were not to be protected from the 'full rigours' of the Government's policy.[34]

3. Small firms and the credit restrictions

One of the aims of the survey conducted by the Oxford Institute of Statistics in 1956 was to determine how important bank lending was to small firms in the manufacturing sector.[35] Unsurprisingly, the most important source of funds for the small firms in the survey was savings derived from past profits. Clearly, the availability of this source of finance depended partly on the profitability of the firm, partly on the amount of tax and finally on the firm's policy with regard to the distribution of profits.[36] The analysis of the finance of expenditure showed that the small firms in the sample were likely to retain profits in order to finance expenditure on operating assets. While on one hand this finding helps support the idea that small firms in the first half of the 1950s relied a great deal on internally generated sources of funds for the provision of their long-term capital, it is necessary to consider whether self-financing might have been, in fact, evidence of financial constraint. Small firms could have been forced to rely heavily on their savings by a scarcity of external finance, therefore trimming their investments to suit these savings. On the strength of this consideration, the survey concluded that the growth of small firms was probably inhibited by the lack of sources of long-term external funds.[37] This conclusion was reinforced by the discovery that the most rapidly expanding firms in the survey were those that relied less on internally generated funds, while the slow growing firms were self-financed.[38]

The survey also established the various sources of external finance available to small firms and, again unsurprisingly, the main source proved to be bank overdrafts. While bank credit was understood to be short-term in nature, its availability allowed firms to free savings for long-term investments. While in the 1950s only 35% of public companies had overdrafts, 47% of the small firms in the Survey had overdrafts and on average these overdrafts represented almost 20% of net assets, twice the average for quoted companies.[39] Small firms also tended to have overdrafts for longer than quoted companies. Most interestingly, the survey revealed how the younger firms in the sample (those founded after 1940) made extensive use of bank loans, compared with firms funded before the Second World War, showing how small, young and rapidly growing firms were more dependent on borrowing from the banks.[40] These results show the crucial role that banks could play in the 'life-cycle' of small firms. In its infancy a small firm's growth potential (and hence its potential for innovation) could be seriously damaged by any curtailment in bank lending.

Part of the Oxford Survey was dedicated to establishing the impact of the credit restrictions between 1950 and 1956 on a sample of small and medium-sized manufacturing firms, none of which were quoted on the Stock Exchange. During this period, of the firms in the sample 35% had been obliged to order less capital equipment than originally planned and/or reduce stocks of materials and parts. The two main reasons given for this reduction were the difficulty of raising finance (43%) and the fear that the credit restrictions would reduce demand, and therefore, sales (46%). For most (72%) of those firms who had been forced to reduce investment plans and/or stock because of the difficulty of raising finance, the main problem was not the higher cost due to increased interest rates but the availability of finance. In other words, of the 876 firms who replied to questions concerning the impact of the credit restrictions, more than 10% had had to reduce their expansion because of the difficulty of raising money. Interestingly, the survey shows how, within the sample, the smaller firms (employing less than 75 people) were more affected by financial difficulties induced by the credit restrictions, while the bigger firms were more concerned with the possible drop in sales, demonstrating the biased nature of the restrictions, a bias that has not been highlighted in the literature on this subject.[41] By focusing on bank lending, the credit restrictions inevitably affected small firms more than large ones, as these had recourse to other sources of finance, such as the capital market.

In their evidence to the Radcliffe Committee, the representatives of the Association of British Chambers of Commerce (hereafter, ABCC) stated that from the onset the effect of the credit restrictions had been more serious for 'small firms and particularly [for] progressive and expanding companies'. Growth-oriented small firms had been particularly affected because 'restriction of bank advances [had] an appreciable effect on plans for capital extension or replacements. Doubts as to the availability of bank credit [led] to the abandonment of schemes for capital expansion'. Small firms were singled out by government policy as their borrowing was confined to bank loans, and though these were not normally used for medium-long term projects the ABCC confirmed that this had become the norm by the second part of the 1950s.[42]

To back up the reports collected from its membership, the Association carried out a survey to ascertain the extent of the impact of the credit restrictions on their membership since 1957. In March 1958, questionnaires were sent out to individual member companies through seventy-two affiliated Chambers of Commerce, and by mid April 3,404 answers had been returned.[43] The findings of the survey allowed the ABCC to support the more impressionistic evidence that the Association had collected for the 1951–56 period: small companies were more adversely affected by the credit squeeze than large ones, as detailed by Table 3.1.

Table 3.1 shows how on all counts the firms employing less than 250 people were those that experienced the most difficulties, while the firms employing less than 100 people were those most affected by the banks' reduction in lending. The smaller firms were also those to resort more to sources of short-term finance other than banks and to purchase machinery using hire purchase.

The results of the ABCC survey mirrored those from an earlier survey carried out in October 1957 by the Birmingham Chamber of Commerce. Table 3.2 was tabulated using answers from 610 manufacturing firms.

Table 3.2 shows that out of a total of 610 members, 42% had experienced a reduction in turnover since 1955, and that the reduction was more marked in the case of firms with capital of less than £100,000. The main reasons given for this reduction were: increased competition, tightness of money among customers, hire purchase restrictions and shortage of capital. The restrictions on borrowing affected firms

Table 3.1 Survey by the Association of British Chambers of Commerce – March 1958

To the general question: 'Have you since September 1957 experienced':
(percentage of replies saying 'yes')

Size of firms (by employment)	Under 100	100–250	250–1000	Over 1000
Turnover reduced	58	51	50	39
Stocks or work in progress reduced	43	37	31	21
Fixed investment projects reduced	24	25	25	23
Fixed investment projects postponed	31	35	34	30
Asked to reduce overdraft*	16	13	8	8
Had overdraft reduced*	14	11	8	7
Taken steps to reduce overdraft*	31	30	29	28
Other short-term finance obtained	7	8	6	3
Machinery purchased on instalment terms	6	9	4	5
Credit squeeze affected ability to carry out export business	10	8	6	3
Forecast contraction for 1958	46	44	42	33

Source: Radcliffe Committee, *Memoranda of evidence*, vol. 2, p. 89.

Note:* This per cent is an underestimate as the Association calculated that at least 25% of firms did not have an overdraft.

Table 3.2 Summary of main findings from Birmingham Chamber of Commerce questionnaire

Percentage of members who between 1955 and 1957 had:

Size of firm by capital	Under £10,000	Under £100,000	Under £250,000	Over £,250,000	Total
Turnover reduced	42%	49%	33%	28%	42%
Overdrafts seriously restricted	13%	10%	7%	9%	10%
Used alternative sources of finance	6.5%	4%	4%	5%	5%
Postponed or cancelled plans since 1955	38.5%	29%	23%	24%	30%
Total number of questionnaires returned	184	252	94	80	610

Source: Radcliffe Committee, *Memoranda of evidence*, vol. 2, p. 88.

differently, depending on their size. Of the smaller firms (those with less than £100,000 capital), 23% had their overdrafts seriously restricted while the larger firms suffered to a lesser extent. More small firms had to postpone or cancel plans for expansion than large firms. Of these postponed plans, almost half were intended to promote exports either directly or indirectly, showing how, in this case at least, the credit restrictions were achieving quite the opposite to the government's aim of improving the balance of payments.[44]

The Federation of British Industry gave evidence on the impact of the restrictions to the Radcliffe Committee, on the strength of 1,595 replies to its questionnaire.[45] The questionnaire sought to establish members' reactions to the government's monetary and fiscal policies, including the credit squeeze during the period 1955–57.[46] The questionnaire was extensive, but Table 3.3 focuses on the relationship between firms and banks.

The evidence from the FBI is useful because it confirms how the impact of the credit squeeze on overdrafts appears to have been inversely proportional to the size of the firms. Of the firms that were required to reduce their existing overdraft limit, 47% employed less than 200 people and of those who were asked to reduce their overdrafts 60% were small firms, while 64% were refused an increase. Conversely, only 28% of the firms whose requirements had been met in full were small firms. The results of these three surveys indicate that monetary policy, in the form of credit restrictions, did not affect all firms in the same way. In fact, the paper submitted to the Committee by the FBI stated that 'the impact of the credit squeeze on overdrafts appears to decrease as the size of the firm increases. The requirements of the larger firms have been very fully met'.[47]

Table 3.3 Survey by the Federation of British Industry:
Percentage of firms who gave affirmative replies for 2 financial years *ending* 1956 to the question: 'If, at any time since the *beginning* of the calendar year 1955, your company has had overdraft facilities, what action did the bank take?'

	All firms	Firms with<200 people
Required to reduce overdraft limit	24%	47%
Required to reduce overdraft	10%	60%
Refused an increase	9%	64%
Requirements met in full	49%	28%

Source: Radcliffe Committee, *Memoranda of evidence*, vol. 2, p. 120.

Two of the industrial associations that gave evidence to the Radcliffe Committee were bodies that represented mainly small firms. One of these was the National Union of Manufacturers. In 1958, the NUM had a membership of more than 5,000 firms, mainly small and medium-sized, and its recognised function was to represent the views and interests of such firms. The evidence presented to the Radcliffe Committee was collected primarily from the smaller firms (mainly employing less than 50 people).[48] In the memoranda submitted to the Committee, the NUM recounted how 'when a small firm needed finance, it always turned to its Bank, relying on the local Manager's knowledge of local affairs to assure him that the risk was a good one and confident that his agreement was all that was needed to secure an overdraft. Few old established firms have not in their early years been saved by the help of a long-sighted bank manager'.

According to the NUM, the credit restrictions had 'seriously curtailed this traditional, flexible and convenient method of finance; and it had operated much more to the detriment of the smaller firm than to that of the bigger. The restrictions had seriously impaired a traditional, and certainly valuable, part of the local business system. That the Banks have reduced their overdraft facilities, and that this has affected mainly the smaller firm, there is no doubt; and it is further true that many firms, in circumstances in which they would have normally have approached their bank, have not done so for fear of a rebuff'.[49]

The NUM, though strongly deploring the impact of the restrictions on the relationship between local bank managers and local businesses, revealed how the curtailment of borrowing had made little difference to the smaller firms' willingness and ability to borrow as they were able to negotiate loans from finance houses, but at considerably higher rates of interest (up to 20% per annum). Thus, the main effect of the credit squeeze had been to force borrowers to pay higher rates of interest than would otherwise be necessary. A higher rate of interest was not regarded by the small firms as an adequate reason for not borrowing, but just as one among many increased costs to be passed on, as far as possible, in higher prices,[50] thus defeating the Government's aim in imposing the credit restrictions reducing inflation. Furthermore, the existence of alternative sources of finance blunted the effectiveness of restricting bank advances as a policy instrument, showing what a narrow view of the operation of the monetary system the authorities had.[51]

The point that small firms' ability to invest had suffered from the restrictions was made at length in the evidence presented by the Engineering Industries Association (hereafter, EIA). The EIA had a membership of 3,500 firms of all sizes, representative of most sections of the engineering industry in Britain. The Association told the Committee how the credit restrictions had led many small and medium sized businesses to postpone or cancel plans for new plant. Successive 'squeezes' had made it clear that it was not safe to rely on bank overdrafts as a means for financial expansion. Though the banks' business was not to supply permanent capital, small engineering firms would nonetheless use overdraft facilities for capital purposes, particularly for the acquisition of plant and machinery.[52] In times of prosperity, a small engineering firm would use 'five or ten thousand pounds' of its overdraft to finance projects such as factory extensions, in the knowledge that the project would be amortised out of the profits made following expansion and the banks were prepared to accept the firm's point of view.[53] Prior to the credit squeeze, the banks were prepared to 'roll-over' the loans they made for periods longer than five years.[54] A 'tremendous number of small and medium-sized engineers' relied on bank overdrafts, and furthermore in most cases the companies with overdrafts were the ones that wanted to expand.[55] Therefore, the curtailment of overdraft extensions had discouraged many small and medium-sized firms from even considering expansion, and they had been forced to 'make do' with machinery which ought to have been replaced, to the extent that these firms felt that 'they were being prevented from increasing their efficiency'. Not surprisingly, small firms blamed the credit restrictions, as these were hindering them 'from offering genuine competition in markets which [were] monopolised by larger producers who, because of their age, [had] financial resources which [were] not available to the smaller and younger firms'.[56] Though the small firms might have been prone to exaggerate the effect of the squeeze on their competitiveness, the Association was apprehensive that Britain was damaging its productive efficiency by continuing credit restrictions too long and adversely affecting fixed capital accumulation: output was being maintained without the requisite modernisation of plant taking place.[57]

4. Small firms and the Macmillan Gap

By reducing the supply of funds available in the economy, the credit restrictions were a contingent factor that inadvertently worsened an existing problem: the gap in the market for the provision of finance to small firms for capital investment. Despite the joint effort of the government and the banks, with the creation of the Industrial Commercial & Finance Corporation (ICFC) in 1945, the Macmillan Gap had not disappeared.

The Association of British Chambers of Commerce revealed to the Radcliffe Committee how evidence collected from its membership showed that there was demand for medium-long term capital that was not being satisfied by ICFC. One of the reasons why demand was not being satisfied was not because firms failed to offer worthwhile projects, but because the resources of ICFC were limited. This was confirmed by the statement of the Chairman of ICFC, Lord Piercy, in presenting the accounts of the Corporation for the year ending March 1957. In Piercy's words, 'the volume of investment was maintained at a high level, but the Corporation was short of funds to deal with all the applications which might justifiably [have been] accepted'.[58] The number of customers on the Corporation's books at 31st March 1958 was only 629 and a total of £56 million had been invested. Piercy himself felt that this was not enough, but also that it was as much that ICFC could do within the statutory constraints put on its resources, and when asked by the Radcliffe Committee whether he thought the MacMillan Gap still existed he answered in the affirmative.[59] It was in Piercy's interest to paint a negative picture, as his aim was to convince the government to allow ICFC to raise part of its funds in the market, thus reducing the banks' control over it. Nevertheless, his views were echoed by the Chambers of Commerce, as these felt that the provision of finance for small firms, especially new and expanding ones, was not adequate to the volume of demand and that if some more comprehensive and adequate form of finance could be established, worthwhile projects would be carried out.[60] The development of a more comprehensive form of finance would have been of great assistance to the very many private companies which '[played] such a vital role in the country's economy and [were] hampered in their development through the lack of adequate finance'.[61] This difficulty was particularly felt by small firms, as these had no other outside source of finance except for the banks, and if these could not accommodate such companies either because of the limitation on advances or the perceived risky nature of the business, then small firms would remain bereft of capital. The ABCC claimed that, '[i]t is becoming more and more difficult to find the necessary financial backing to start up a new venture which cannot offer much security, but which may hold out great promise for long-term development, i.e. the form of risk capital which was provided by private individuals in the past and which was without doubt the foundation of many of the large and prosperous businesses of today'.[62]

Furthermore, ICFC was not known by many firms, and '[a]lthough they may have been sent documents, it is much more natural for them to go to their bank manager with whom they have done business for years, whom they know and trust. They are timid. A lot of small businesses shrink away from coming to a finance house in London, if they can borrow from their own bank'.[63] Despite the fact that ICFC had regional offices at the time, this was not sufficient to make it known to small firms.[64]

The findings of the Oxford Survey provide further evidence that during the 1950s there were many small firms that could not, or would not, deal with ICFC. Respondents to the Survey were asked whether over the period 1950–56 they had ever '. . . tried to get funds from any other institutions specialising in the finance of small and medium sized businesses' [such as ICFC]. Of the 1,021 firms who answered this question, 95% had not tried, 1% had tried and succeeded, and 3.6% had tried and been rejected. Of the firms who had not tried, 50% had not heard of such institutions and the other 50% did not want any interference.[65] Moreover, one of the problems encountered by ICFC in making itself known to potential customers was the reluctance of the banks in advertising the Corporation's activities, a reluctance due to the fear of losing potential customers and in the case of some branches, ignorance.[66]

In its concluding report, the Radcliffe Committee commented on the situation in the following terms: '. . . there is a danger, which it is socially and economically desirable to avoid, that the growth of small firms may be impeded because they lack some of the facilities open to large companies for obtaining capital'.[67] The Committee concluded that the Mac-Millan Gap had not been bridged as in the main small firms, and new entrepreneurs could only use their banks as a source of finance. During the 1950s, the problem was compounded by the government's policy of restricting credit, since small firms – that category of firms that had no other source of external funds except for banks – suffered a decrease in the availability of bank loans.[68]

5. Small firms and hire purchase

The evidence generated by the firms, presented in the above pages, shows that these firms thought the credit restrictions were hindering their investment plans, and therefore their competitiveness. Or at least this is what firms *said*. The view could be taken that it was in businesses' interest to make themselves heard and therefore what they said did not necessarily reflect reality. In conditions of uncertainty, moreover, it might have been entirely rational not to engage in costly investments. This paper shows that in terms of general welfare the government's use of monetary policy for macroeconomic purposes had a negative impact, as it generated uncertainty. However, the British economy in the 1950s was growing at an unprecedented rate and the following pages show how, despite uncertainty over the availability of bank loans, some small firms chose not to wait, but instead exercised their option to invest by using an alternative source of finance.[69]

The strategy adopted by small firms to exercise their option to invest and to bridge to some extent the Macmillan Gap, inadvertently widened by the government through the credit restrictions, was to make use of hire purchase to acquire plant and machinery to a much greater extent than ever before. Table 3.4 below shows the sources of finance, alternative to banks, used by firms since the tightening of the restrictions.

Of the various alternatives to banks, the finance houses proved to be the most popular, especially for those firms employing less than 250 people. The primary function of the finance houses was to provide medium term finance (from 6 months to 3 years) for the acquisition of industrial and agricultural machinery, plant, motor vehicles, furniture and other domestic goods.[70] In 1959, 8–10% of their business was in industrial equipment,[71] 70% was credit on motor vehicles,[72] while the rest would have been for consumer credit. At the request of its customer, the finance house would buy specific goods for which it would pay the full retail price and which it would then hire to the customer under a hire purchase agreement. In 1957, there were more than 1,000 finance houses, though most of the credit agreements were concentrated in the hands of nine.[73]

In the second part of the 1950s, the effective interest rate charged on hire purchase was 15–20% on a reducing balance.[74] Apart from the security offered by the deposit, the potential customer's financial standing was checked very carefully as the finance houses did not want to rely on

Table 3.4 Survey by the Association of British Chambers of Commerce – March 1958

To the question: Since September 1957 have you sought and obtained short-term finance (which you would otherwise have sought or obtained from a bank) from alternative sources? (percentage of replies saying 'yes')

Source of finance	Size of firms			
	Under 100	100–250	250–1000	Over 1000
Finance companies	42	62	49	50
Insurance companies	8	7	10	12
Building societies	13	2	–	13
Other specified sources	37	29	41	25

Source: Radcliffe Committee, *Memoranda*, vol. 2, pp. 92–93.

re-possession, especially with machinery and machine tools, as it would have been very difficult to re-possess and re-sell.[75] In the late 1950s, typical bad loss figures were '0.13 of one per cent of turnover'.[76] Such low bad debt is not surprising: the firms who relied on hire purchase usually already had an overdraft and had therefore passed the banks' stringent criteria of creditworthiness. In fact, bank references were called up when new customers approached a finance house; in the case of those firms who did not have overdrafts, two local references were asked for, usually from tradesmen who had done business with the firm.[77] The terms of the hire would vary from case to case, but typically the customer would be required to make equal monthly payments over a period varying between 12 and 24 months. The latter period was the maximum permitted by the Board of Trade in 1958 for plant and machinery, while in the absence of controls the periods of payments for this category of goods would have varied between 3 and 5 years.[78] To obviate the time restriction and meet the growing demand from firms, the finance houses developed an innovative way of doing business for goods that normally would have required periods longer than 24 months to be paid off. For example, in the case of the financing for open-cast coal mining, the price of machinery was between £60,000 and £100,000 per unit. As it would have been very costly to pay for such machinery over two years, the finance houses would simply hire the machinery to the company, which never owned it but would pay monthly rent for it until it was time to replace it, while charging the whole of these payments to tax.[79] Hire purchase was very easy to arrange, especially for a creditworthy firm (creditworthiness would be signalled by the firm already having an overdraft), and it had the additional advantage of not requiring security (as the ownership of the good by the finance house was security in itself), but it was much more expensive than bank charges, 15–20% on a reducing balance compared to 5–7% charged by the banks.[80]

The Oxford survey gives a clear picture of the use of hire purchase by small manufacturing firms. The most interesting finding of the survey was that hire purchase was used more by the smaller firms in the sample and by firms that already had an overdraft. In fact, after overdrafts H.P. was the most commonly used source of external finance for this size of firm.[81] Fifty per cent of the firms that had an overdraft all or most of the time used H.P., while only 15% of firms without an overdraft used H.P.[82] Furthermore, H.P. was more likely to be used by the rapidly growing firms in the sample, especially in the engineering sector for the purchase of machine tools, as these were easily financed by a hire purchase agreement.[83] Although frequently used, H.P. accounted for a small part of the finance raised by small firms,[84] indicating that it was used in those cases when extension of plant and purchase of machinery was needed but the bank would not extend credit.

The finance houses did not escape the Treasury's notice and restrictions were imposed on the terms of hire purchase in 1952 when the minimum deposit on consumer goods, including motor vehicles, was increased to 33 per cent and the hire period reduced to 18 months. In the summer of 1954, all controls were lifted, only to be reinstated in February 1955, but in 'softer' terms: the minimum deposit was reduced to 15 per cent and the hire period extended to 24 months. A year later, the controls were tightened, the minimum deposit increased to 50 per cent of the value of the purchased good and for the first time the controls were extended to finance on industrial plant and machinery. The controls were kept in place until October of 1958.[85] The restrictions on hire purchase finance had a double effect that, in the view of the Engineering Industries Association, was worse than the bank credit restrictions. Firstly, the frequent alterations of policy caused violent fluctuations in the demand for finished goods and this interfered with the flow of production of subcontractors and manufacturers of components. Secondly, the restrictions on hire purchase, relating to capital equipment, caused many firms to refrain from embarking upon modernisation and expansion of their plant since 'owing to the shortage of capital facilities engineering firms [had] resorted to hire purchase for the acquisition of machinery'.[86]

Nevertheless, in the second half of the 1950s, the need for funds was such that, despite its cost, and the government's restrictions, H.P. on industrial equipment increased rapidly. There are no published yearly figures for new H.P. credit extended directly to hirers for plant and machinery by finance houses in the 1950s, except for December 1957 when this was estimated to have been in the order of £17 million.[87] In 1955, however, the *Board of Trade Journal* started publishing index numbers of new H.P. on plant and machinery extended by finance houses per calendar month: using these indices it is possible to calculate a series of values of H.P. from December 1955 to December 1959.[88] These estimates are shown in the first column in Table 3.1 in the appendix to the paper. The Oxford survey calculated that at the beginning of 1956, H.P. on plant and machinery taken on by small and medium sized firms would have been about £7 million;[89] Table 3.1 in the appendix shows that total H.P. on plant and machinery extended in 1955 was £11.4 million, and by using the Oxford Survey figure we can estimate that well over 50% of H.P. for this category of goods was being used by small firms. By assuming this percent as constant,[90] it is possible to estimate the increase in

H.P. on plant and machinery taken on by small firms between 1955 and 1959. The second column of figures in Table 3.1 in the appendix shows how in the three years between December 1955 and December 1958 the use of hire purchase by small firms doubled.[91] Following the end of the credit squeeze, the steep rise in the use of hire purchase between October 1958 and December 1959 reveals the extent of pent-up demand for finance.

Conclusion

This paper has shown that by combining 'supply-side' and 'demand-side' evidence to study the financial difficulties of small firms in the 1950s, it is possible to add another dimension to the debate on the impact of 'stop-go' policies on the micro-economy. Using a number of sources, the paper has shown how in the 1950s, small, innovative firms were those likely to have an overdraft, and to use this overdraft to finance their expansion. The credit restrictions imposed by the government as part of their monetary policy forced the banks to reduce all overdrafts, but it was the smaller customers who bore the brunt of the banks' rationing strategy. Since overdrafts were used for capital purposes, it can be said that the actions of the government not only singled out one particular sector of the economy, but also widened the 'MacMillan Gap'. The small firms' response was to finance plant and machinery by increasing their use of hire purchase, a costly and rather inflexible form of finance as it required a large deposit and allowed only a short repayment period.

Treasury officials and Ministers believed that direct lending controls would have an effect on monetary conditions. In fact, these controls led to increasing levels of disintermediation, as institutions such as the finance houses, not affected by credit ceilings, were given an artificial advantage over the commercial banks. This lack of understanding on the part of policy makers not only led to a substantial section of British industry being forced into borrowing capital in an inefficient way, but also to the commercial banks being turned into a declining public utility whose only role was to say 'no'.[92]

The sources used for this paper show that the firms who used overdrafts and hire purchase were more likely to be young and dynamic and the link between external finance and growth is confirmed by a later study funded by the Social Science Research Council on a sample of small firms. This study found that there was a strong relationship between financial postures and the performance, and aims, of a company. Those firms that did not complain of financial problems were also more likely to be liquid, satisfied with their performance and size and to have rather restricted aims, while those firms whose chief executives described their financial problems as an obstacle to progress were in the top third in terms of growth performance. These firms were also thinking of expanding their business over the following five years and were already borrowing from other sources.[93] *Ceteris paribus*, the transition from small to medium-sized seems to rest on the availability of external finance, and Britain's poor performance in terms of the relative low level of output accounted for by medium-sized enterprises compared to other countries suggests the existence of barriers to growth that prevent the transition to larger scales of successful competitive activity.[94] The evidence presented in this paper indicates that the historical study of how small firms financed their activities, and of how the issue of finance was perceived by the institutions that governed the economy, can shed some light on the nature of these barriers.

Notes

* This paper has greatly benefited from comments by Sue Bowden, Andrew Priest, Peter Scott, Jim Tomlinson and Katherine Watson; to them go all my gratitude for their support and help. I also wish to thank the two anonymous referees for their comments and suggestions. All remaining mistakes are of course mine.

1 By 1965, 88 per cent of British households had a television, 56 per cent were equipped with washing machines and 39 per cent with refrigerators; in 1964 three-fifths of the population were taking their holidays away from home. D. Childs, *Britain since 1945* (London: Routledge, 1992), pp. 105–106.

2 M. D. Bordo & B. Eichengreen, *A retrospective on the Bretton Woods System* (Cambridge, MA: Chigago University Press, 1993).

3 See: A. Shonfield, *British economic policy since the war* (Harmondsworth: Penguin Books, 1958), J. C. R. Dow, *The management of the British Economy* (Cambridge: Cambridge University Press, 1970); and more recently J. Tomlinson, *British macroeconomic policy since 1940* (London: Croom Helm, 1985).

4 For a contemporary assessment of the banks' contribution to small firms financing in the 1950s see: Lord Piercy, 'The MacMillan Gap and the shortage of risk capital', *Journal of the Royal Statistical Society*, vol. 118 (1955), part 1, p. 4.

5 In 1931 the Committee on Finance and Industry, chaired by Harold Macmillan, noted that 'It has been represented to us that great difficulty is experienced by the smaller and mediumsized businesses in raising . . . capital . . . even when the security offered is perfectly sound' (British Parliamentary Papers, Cmd. 3897, Committee on Finance and Industry, *Report*, para. 404.).

6 This is not to detract from the work currently being undertaken on the finance houses and credit for consumer durables, see: S. Bowden, 'Collusion and

competition in the finance sector in the post-war period', *Financial History Review*, 4 (1997), pp. 161–179; for hire purchase financing in the inter-war period see: S. Bowden, M. Collins, ' The Bank of England, industrial regeneration and hire purchase between the wars', *Economic History Review*, XLV (1992), no. 1, pp. 120–136.

7 The results of the survey were published in a number of academic journals between 1956 and 1962 and collected in J. Bates, *The financing of small businesses* (London: Sweet & Maxwell, 1964).

8 In 1958 enterprises employing less than 200 people accounted for 24% of total employment, and for 20% of total net output, but these shares had declined from 38% and 35% respectively in 1935. Over the same period the number of small enterprises had fallen from 136,000 to 66,000. British Parliamentary Papers, Committee of Inquiry on Small Firms, Cmnd. 4811, 1971–72, pp. 58–60 and 68–70. (Hereafter Bolton Committee).

9 Bolton Committee, *Research Report no. 6*.

10 E. Penrose, *The theory of the growth of the firm* (Basil Blackwell, Oxford, 1968), pp. 222–228.

11 M. Amendola & J. Gaffard, *The innovative choice* (Oxford: Basil Blackwell, 1988), pp. 40–43.

12 J. Tomlinson, 'Conservative Modernisation, 1960–64: Too Little, Too late?', *Contemporary British History*, vol. 11, no. 3 (Autumn 1997), pp. 18–38.

13 The findings of the Bolton Committee were confirmed by other, later studies: see P. Geroski, *Market structure, corporate performance and innovative activity* (Oxford: Clarendon Press, 1994).

14 HMSO, *Employment Policy White Paper*, 1944, p. 1.

15 *House of Commons Debates*, 10 April, 1951, cols. 841–2.

16 Bank of England Archive (hereafter BEA), Chief Cashier Private Files, 7/11/1951, C40/687. The first rise in the Bank rate since 1939 occurred in November 1951 when it was increased by half a per cent. to 2.5. After that first rise changes to the rate were always included with the other elements of monetary policy. Between November 1951 and November 1958 Bank rate rose, or fell, 13 times, reaching its highest rate at 7 per cent. in September 1957. See: J. C. R. Dow, *The management of the British economy 1945–60* (Cambridge: Cambridge University Press, 1970), p. 253.

17 Quarterly figures (in current terms) from Bank of England, *Statistical Abstract*.

18 BEA, Chief Cashier Private Files, 2/11/1952, C40/687.

19 BEA, Chief Cashier Private Files, Reports from Midland, Westminster, Lloyds and Barcays, 22/7/1952, C40/687.

20 *House of Commons Debates*, 19 April 1955, cols. 55–6.

21 BEA, Statement sent by the Chancellor to the Bank, C40/689.

22 BEA, Minutes of meeting of Committee of London Clearing Banks, 26/7/1955, and Report on advances, 31/10/1955, C 40/689.

23 BEA, Report on advances, quarterly figures, 16/8/1955, C40/689.

24 BEA, Governor's note on interviews with bankers, 3/10/1955, C40/689.

25 G. D. N. Worswick & P. H. Ady (eds), *The British economy in the 1950s* (Oxford: Clarendon Press, 1962), p. 305.

26 Dow, *The management of the British economy 1945–60*, p. 255.

27 BEA, Advances and the control of inflation files, 12 July 1949, C40/686.

28 Long term series of figures for advances (in current terms) can be found in: Bank of England, *Statistical Abstract* (1970), vol. 1, pp. 68–70.
29 Lloyds Bank Archive, Sir Oliver Franks, 'Bank advances as an object of policy', Winton File, 1950, pp. 5–6.
30 BEA, Confidential reports from the banks, 16/3/1956, C40/691.
31 BEA, Memo on the number of bankruptcies, 12/9/1956, C40/692.
32 With the proviso that bankruptcy figures are difficult to interpret due to the obvious problem of establishing a correct lag period, it should be noted that their number for the manufacturing sector (businesses and individuals) had increased steadily from 1945 and between 1955 and 1956 had risen by 14%. However, between 1956 and 1959 the number of bankruptcies fell slightly, by about 5%, only to rise steadily again until 1963. The number of bankruptcies in 1960 was 17% higher than it had been ten years earlier. Nevertheless, the absolute number of bankruptcies in the manufacturing sector remained small (177 in 1950, 207 in 1960), compared with the total number of firms in the economy. However, the number of firms being forced into liquidation by the credit restrictions might have been higher. Indeed the secondary literature on small firms and finance does make this connection. The absence of data on the liquidation of unincorporated firms (most small firms) in this period makes it impossible to test this hypothesis. The bankruptcy figures are taken from: Board Of Trade, *Bankruptcy. General Annual Reports* (HMSO, 1949–1963).
33 Only those firms who figured as exporters were supposed to receive advances from their banks.
34 *Hansard*, vol. 554, 1413–1425, 28 July 1955.
35 For a full analysis of the sample and methodology used in the Small Businesses survey see: Bates, *The financing of small businesses*, Appendix A.
36 Bates, *The financing of small businesses*, p. 36.
37 Bates, *The financing of small businesses*, pp. 27–28.
38 Bates, *The financing of small businesses*, pp. 56–57.
39 B. Tew, R. F. Henderson, *Studies in company finance* (Cambridge: Cambridge University Press, 1959), p. 90–91.
40 Bates, *The financing of small businesses*, pp. 90–93.
41 The sample used in the survey was considered to be representative of all British manufacturing firms within the size limit of 11–499 employees. For a description of the sample and a more extensive analysis of the survey's findings, see: H. F. Lydall, 'The impact of the credit squeeze on small and medium-sized firms', *Economic Journal*, vol. LXVII (1957).
42 Committee on the working of the monetary system (hereafter Radcliffe), Cmnd 827, *Memoranda of evidence*, vol. 2, p. 85.
43 Distribution of answers by employment size: 1679 firms employed less than 100 people; 725 employed between 100–250 people; 685 employed between 250–1000 people while 315 employed over 1000 people; this distribution of firms is not surprising as the membership of the Chambers of Commerce reflected more closely the distribution of firms in the economy than the Federation of British Industry did, since the majority of its members were large firms, see Footnote no. 38. The Survey was taken at the end of what the Association termed 'a classic period in [the] recent monetary history', the 6 months from September 1957 to March 1958 when the Bank Rate stood at 7%. See: Radcliffe, *Memoranda*, p. 88.

44 Radcliffe, *Memoranda*, vol. 2, p. 88.
45 Distribution of answers by employment size of the firms: 593 employed less than 200 people, 447 employed between 200 and 700, while 555 employed more than 700 people. Unsurprisingly the majority of firms that returned the questionnaire were medium-large, public companies; this was not representative of the structure of British industry but rather of the membership of the FBI. In all three surveys, ABCC, Birmingham Chamber of Commerce and FBI, the answers represented between 20–25% of the total number of questionnaires sent.
46 The following figures are different from the ones published in the memoranda of evidence because these calculated percentages on the total number of questionnaires returned. The estimates presented here are based on the total who in fact answered the questions.
47 Radcliffe, *Memoranda*, vol. 2, p. 118.
48 Radcliffe, *Memoranda*, vol. 2, pp. 137–138.
49 Radcliffe, *Memoranda*, vol. 2, p. 137.
50 Radcliffe, *Memoranda*, vol. 2, p. 137.
51 D. Ross, 'British monetary policy and the banking system in the 1950s', *Business and Economic History*, vol. 21 (1992), p. 205.
52 Radcliffe, *Memoranda*, vol. 2, p. 108.
53 Radcliffe, *Minutes*, qn. 6330.
54 Radcliffe, *Minutes*, qn. 6333.
55 Radcliffe, *Minutes*, qn. 6335.
56 Radcliffe, *Memoranda*, vol. 2, p. 108.
57 Radliffe, *Minutes*, qn. 6352.
58 Radcliffe, *Memoranda*, vol. 2, p. 86.
59 Radcliffe, *Memoranda*, vol. 3 , p. 198.
60 This point was also made by the Engineering Industries Association who pointed out that while the 'Macmillan Gap' might have become smaller due to the introduction of institutions such as ICFC, the main need was for a body which could provide relatively small sums (up to £10,000) for start-up businesses on a 3–7 year loan. The spokesman for the EIA suggested that this need could be met by industrial banks 'on the continental model' or by local finance companies, with officers familiar with local conditions, to replace the loss of the wealthy local investor of pre-war memory. See: Radcliffe, *Memoranda*, vol. 2, p. 110 and *Minutes*, qn. 6404.
61 Radcliffe, *Memoranda*, vol. 2, p. 86.
62 Radcliffe, *Memoranda*, vol. 2, p. 86.
63 Radcliffe, *Minutes*, qn. 11123.
64 Radcliffe, *Minutes*, qn. 11124.
65 Bates, *The financing of small businesses*, p. 79.
66 Radcliffe, *Minutes*, qn. 11123.
67 Radcliffe, *Final Report of the Committee*, para. 932.
68 This point has been made by others interested in the constraints suffered by small firms. Most notably see Penrose, *The theory of the growth of the firm*, p. 219.
69 K. A. Dixit & R. S. Pindyck, *Investment under uncertainty* (Princeton: Princeton University Press, 1994).
70 For an introduction to the history of the Finance Houses and of hire purchase see: R. Harris, M. Naylor, A. Seldon, *Hire Purchase in a Free Society*

(London: Hutchinson & Co. Ltd, 1961). See also the sections on Hire Purchase and Finance Houses in Committee on Consumer Credit (Crowther Committee), Cmnd. 4596, *Report*, vol. 1 (1971), pp. 42–46 and pp. 66–74.

71 Radcliffe, *Minutes*, qns. 5177–5178.

72 For an assessment of the role played by the Finance Houses in the growth of domestic demand for motor vehicles, see S. Bowden, 'Competition and collusion in the finance sector in the post-war period', *Financial History Review*, n. 4 (1997).

73 Harris, Naylor, Seldon, *Hire Purchase*, p. 40.

74 Bates, *The financing of small businesses*, p. 127.

75 Radcliffe, *Minutes*, qn. 5155.

76 Bad loss figures were calculated as follows: losses written off = net loss after taking credit for re-sale of re-possessed goods. See: Radcliffe, *Minutes*, qn. 5170.

77 V. R. Fox-Smith, *Hire Purchase, Credit and Finance* (London: Stevens, 1962), p. 23.

78 Radcliffe, *Memoranda*, p. 27.

79 Radcliffe, *Minutes*, qns. 5144 and 5149.

80 Bates, 'Hire purchase', p. 275 and p. 279.

81 J. A. Bates, 'Hire purchase in small manufacturing businesses', *The Bankers' Magazine* (1957), p. 177.

82 Bates, *The financing of small businesses*, p. 121.

83 Bates, 'Hire purchase', p. 175 and pp. 275–276.

84 Nevertheless H.P. was never a very high percentage of current liabilities; in 70% of the firms in the sample H.P. outstanding accounted for less than 10% of current liabilities. See: Bates, 'Hire purchase', p. 278.

85 Radcliffe, *Memoranda*, p. 29.

86 Radcliffe, *Memoranda*, p. 109 and *Minutes*, qn. 6365.

87 *Census of Distribution and other Services*, 1957, table 20.

88 The index based on December 1955 is taken from: *Board of Trade Journal*, 16th August, 1957, p. 359. The index based on July 1957 is taken from: *Board of Trade Journal*, 18th July 1958, p. 123. The Board of Trade estimated that new H.P. for plant and machinery in December 1955 had been 1.05 million pounds.

89 Bates, 'Hire purchase', p. 172. Bates estimates that most of the firms in this category would have employed less than 100 people.

90 This is a very generous underestimate, because as the credit restrictions on bank lending worsened small firms would have resorted more to H.P. as an alternative.

91 Yearly figures for total new H.P. can be calculated by adding up the monthly figures. In fact these aggregate figures are more significant than the monthly ones as these are affected by a certain degree of seasonality.

92 F. Capie, C. Goodhart & S. Fisher, *The future of central banking* (Cambridge: Cambridge University Press, 1994), p. 26.

93 J. Boswell, *The rise and decline of small firms* (London: Allen and Unwin, 1973), pp. 219–222.

94 C. Driver & P. Dunne (eds), *Structural change in the UK economy* (Cambridge: Cambridge University Press, 1992), pp. 100–114.

Appendix I

Table 3.1 Estimates of new hire purchase credit on plant and machinery extended directly to hirers (millions).

All firms and firms employing less than 100 people.

	AH firms	Small firms
Dec – 1955	1.05	0.52
Jan – 1956	1.29	0.64
Feb	1.35	0.67
Mar	0.88	0.44
Apr	0.71	0.35
May	0.79	0.39
Jun	0.91	0.45
Jul	0.87	0.43
Aug	0.89	0.44
Sept	0.89	0.44
Oct	0.87	0.43
Nov	1.06	0.53
Dec	0.86	0.43
Jan – 1957	1.16	0.58
Feb	1.06	0.53
Mar	1.05	0.52
Apr	1.33	0.66
May	1.22	0.61
Jun	1.52	0.76
Jul	1.52	0.76
Aug	1.37	0.68
Sept	1.70	0.85
Oct	1.84	0.92
Nov	1.56	0.78
Dec	1.32	0.66
Jan – 1958	1.61	0.80
Feb	1.50	0.75
Mar	1.75	0.87
Apr	1.79	0.89

(Continued)

Table 3.1 (Continued)

	AH firms	Small firms
May	1.82	0.91
Jun	1.41	0.70
Jul	1.81	0.90
Aug	1.30	0.65
Sept	1.35	0.67
Oct	2.16	1.08
Nov	1.93	0.96
Dec	1.90	0.95
Jan – 1959	2.23	1.11
Feb	2.07	1.03
Mar	2.89	1.44
Apr	2.74	1.37
May	2.35	1.17
Jun	2.87	1.43
Jul	3.19	1.59
Aug	2.45	1.22
Sept	2.67	1.33
Oct	2.98	1.49
Nov	2.86	1.43
Dec	2.84	1.42

Source: Data calculated from Board of Trade indices, see footnote 89 for full reference.

Chapter 4

Corporate governance in a political climate

The 'City', the government and British Leyland Motor Corporation*

Sue Bowden

Introduction

As economic historians, we devote much expertise to dissecting the performance of firms, industries and sectors over time and over geographical region, drawing on insights from the economics and management
literatures to help explain revealed behaviour. As such, our discipline
has offered crucial insights into why firms have prospered, how and why
firms have experienced difficulties and how and why changing technolo-
gies, macro-economic environments and individuals may have contributed to success or failure.[1] Less well understood are the mechanisms
whereby a record of under-performance may be reversed.

One obvious route towards a greater understanding of this phoenom-
enon is via the the corporate governance literature. Here we find theoretical insights into the rights and responsibilities of ownership and
empirical findings on the exercise of those responsibilities. The former
is grounded in principal-agent and game theory approaches, the latter in
aggregate analyses of share price behaviour.[2] As such, this literature may
yield insights into the exercise of ownership responsibilities and why
under-performance may not always be corrected.

There are two problems with this literature, which economic historians are well equipped to address. First, the literature is set in a political
vacuum in which the impact of public policy regimes on both owners
and managers is ignored.[3] Second, much of the empirical literature is
grounded in aggregate analyses of share price behaviour in which actual
share transactions behaviour of different shareholders is ignored. It follows that a more fruitful avenue would be to examine share transactions
(and/or other evidence of ownership behaviour) by named shareholders (distinguishing for example between private, insurance, banks, pension fund shareholders) for one company which explicitly builds into

the analysis the effect on strategic choices and behaviour patterns of the prevailing public policy regime.

Fusion of share transactions behaviour with analyses of government archives allows us to examine corporate governance in its appropriate political climate. If to this we add company archives and interviews, we have a rich quantitative and qualitative source base from which we can examine how ownership and managerial responsibilities were exercised, how public policy impacted on behaviour and, ultimately, how and why a record of under-performance may not be corrected.

This paper addresses the failure to correct the under-performance of the British Leyland Motor Corporation (BLMC) from the above perspective. The aim is not to add to the now voluminous literature detailing the misfortunes of the company, but to explore why, given these misfortunes, owners were unable to correct under-performance.[4] Both Church and more recently Whisler have detailed how the company became locked into a prevailing ethos, inherited from Morris, based on an arrogant and mis-placed belief in the superiority of the company's product and an innate assumption that all the company had to do was to make cars.[5] Despite changes in structure and personnel, that ethos was never challenged. The assumption created a situation of path-dependency and lock-in, whereby the dominant ethos continued to dominate managerial strategy, despite structural and personnel changes.

The problem with the path dependency and lock-in thesis of Church and Whisler is that it can be a restrospective justification. It fails to address the crucial issue: why was that ethos never challenged seriously as evidence mounted of the company's problems. Neither Church nor Whisler take on board who (and why) might have challenged such assumptions. As such, the issue of corporate governance is never addressed. This paper tries to ask – and provide some answers – to these questions.

The case study follows from the wealth of primary archives and from the willingness of key protagonists to make available private records and to give interviews. BLMC may be unique in the annals of 'problematic' companies; it is not unique, however, in its persistent inability to address those problems. It was not the only company to be influenced by public policy; nor was it the only company to prompt 'mixed message' reactions by shareholders.[6] One also suspects it will not be the last.

Section I explores key insights from the theoretical literature on corporate governance, and explains why the conventional empirical view stresses major constraints on the realisation of the mechanisms for correcting under-performance in the UK. Section II considers why and how the behaviour of both managers and owners can only be understood fully when placed in the prevailing public policy regime. Section III identifies the bargaining positions, assumptions and constraints faced by each of the key interested parties. It clarifies the extent to which the major shareholders were constrained in the strategies they adopted. Section IV uses revealed share transactions behaviour, in conjunction with interviews with important protagonists and original archival sources, to explain how corporate governance was determined at BLMC. We finish the introduction, however, with a brief overview of the company in question in order to establish the truism that this really was a company in need of intervention to correct blatant under-performance.

Our case study is that of the major British producer of motor vehicles in the post-war period, BLMC. The company in question underwent several reconstructions, with accompanying name changes, between 1952 and 1986.[7] Throughout these years, the performance of the company under its different names was problematic. From the mid 1950s, BMC was overtaken by Ford, in profit terms. The volatility of profit growth, closely related to fluctuations in motor vehicle output, was less of a problem than the overall downward trend and the collapse in profits in the early and mid 1960s.[8] By 1967, BMH was recording negative profits. In 1968, that company merged with Leyland to form BLMC, but the merger failed to realise its objective of reversing the company's fortunes. The performance of BLMC during its short lifetime was, to say the least, unimpressive: volatile and at times declining output growth and low and ultimately negative profit growth (Table 4.1) were symptomatic of a company experiencing serious difficulties. Here we have a company which, self-evidently, under-performed not only in terms of sales and profits growth but also, and crucially, from the point of view

Table 4.1 Financial Performance of British Leyland Motor Corporation, 1968–1975 (£m)

Year	Total Sales	Exports from UK	Post-Tax Profits	Dividends Paid
1968	907	276	20.30	14.80
1969	970	322	20.80	14.80
1970	1021	351	2.30	5.00
1971	1177	414	18.40	10.80
1972	1281	355	21.10	11.80
1973	1564	424	27.90	8.70
1974	1596	485	-6.70	3.00
1975	1868	589	-63.20	0.00

Source: British Leyland Motor Corporation, Annual Report and Accounts, 1968–1975.

of shareholders, in its apparent inability to maintain dividend growth. In theory, as the corporate governance literature outlined in the next section demonstrates, one might expect shareholders (the ultimate owners of the company) to react.

I

In theory, shareholders, as ultimate owners of a company, constitute the principal. The functions and expectations of the principal are to protect the interests of the shareholders and, as such, to maximise dividend returns and growth. If the performance of the company is such that future dividend streams are believed to be threatened, the principal may take one of two courses of action. The principal may express exit by selling shares in the company or exercise voice by expressing concerns to management with a view to influencing an improvement in the company's performance.[9] What determines which course of action is adopted depends on perceived incentives. The two courses of action are not, of course, mutually exclusive. Whether exit follows failed attempts to express voice depends on perceived incentives.

Exit would be the preferred response from shareholders concerned to protect short-run dividend returns.[10] As such, sales of shares and transfer into holdings of companies deemed to promise better returns might be a sensible course of action. This would be an explanation which would appeal to advocates of a short-termist interpretation of the behaviour of shareholders in UK company stock. Switching of shares to maximise short-run dividend returns might make sense from the perspective of an individual investor, but would put pressure on companies to ensure high and sustained dividend growth. Such a view would see shareholders as abdicating their responsibility to influence management and merely transferring equity to maximise immediate returns: a market in property rights in which investors switch equity according to which stock promises the better returns.[11] In these terms, the principal cedes the onus of any obligation to turn round an under-performing company.

Exit, however, need not be a 'black or white' strategy. A principal wishing to express dis-satisfaction may not choose to express full exit by selling all shares in the company. Limited exit is an option. In this scenario, the principal sells sufficient shares to effect a fall in the market price which makes the company vulnerable to take-over. This gives warning to management that, unless performance is improved, they are at risk of take-over. For this to constitute a real warning, sufficient shares have to be sold. This, however, involves some risk to the principal of driving down the market price and being left with under-valued shares on their portfolio. It also presumes the credibility of the threat that another company might wish to launch a take-over bid.

In the event that a shareholder has large stakes in any one company, the disincentive to exit may overrule any incentive to sell equity. Whilst it might be possible for shareholders with small equity stakes to exit any one company, the risks for large shareholders could outweigh potential gains. In order to protect dividend income, significant selling would be required. Small-scale selling would be insufficient to protect the future dividend stream of the investing shareholder. But large-scale selling would not go unnoticed and could prompt widescale selling which, in turn, would drive down the market price and raise the possibility of the shareholder being left with marked down stock on their portfolio.

If there are disincentives to sell equity, how else might large shareholders behave? *In theory*, the voice option may be exercised.[12] Voice could range from general discussions between management and the principal shareholders, to specific attempts by the latter to get the former to change policy, to attempts to remove either the managing director or the whole board.[13] The first complication is that in practice, more than one institution will hold large equity stakes in any one company.[14] The incentive to exercise voice will depend upon relative bargaining leverages as between these institutions and the disincentives for any one to assume the role of voice whilst others free ride on the benefits of any such intervention. Any attempt to exert influence will cost time and energy and hence money. It presumes that any such shareholder has the expertise, will and, most importantly, sufficient equity to influence management. That any such shareholder would willingly put itself in such a position, with the consequent risks of what happens if performance is not turned round, ignores perceived incentives as between large shareholders.

In theory, the resolution of this predicament is placed on the shoulders and expectations of non-executive directors who sit on the company board as representatives of shareholders and may act as a channel for expressing shareholder dis-satisfaction.[15] The ability to perform such obligations at times of under-performance may be constrained by incentives for such individuals to intervene. Who appoints the non-executive directors will have a direct bearing on their leverage. Appointments made by management rather than shareholders will lead to a disinclination to subject management to serious questioning, as will board meetings which are a formality. If the latter applies, asymmetric information problems apply and the non-executive directors may not be apprised of any more detailed information which lies behind company performance than the shareholders. Equally, the number of non-executive directors will have a bearing on their influence: the fewer there are, the less will be their 'voice'. In the UK, the propensity to have a small number of internally appointed non-executive directors has diminished the effectiveness of this mechanism of corporate governance.

If the route to correcting under-performance lies neither in equity trading nor in intervention by non-executive directors, then, in theory, shareholders can resort to two other internal mechanisms: the carrot of linking pay to performance and the stick of seeking management dismissals. The former presumes that reward systems will act as an incentive for management to improve company performance. This may be effected through salary and /or share incentive schemes, with the latter having the additional benefit of aligning managerial interests with those of shareholders.[16] Share incentive schemes might realign managerial strategies and ensure future dividend streams without necessitating shareholder intervention to change management: a change of interest rather than personnel.

The behaviour of different groups of shareholders as predicted by the theoretical literature assumes a distribution of equity with shareholders having sufficient shares to determine market price and/or managerial performance. Although the distribution of shares did change from small holdings by numerous private individuals towards large block holdings by the financial institutions, shareholding in the UK (as in the USA) is characterised now, and still more so in the pre-Thatcher years, by small widely dispersed shareholdings and unitary boards.[17] The post-war decades witnessed a significant shift in that institutional investors came to provide the vast bulk of the capital going into British industry, but equity holdings by institutional investors were spread throughout industry. In 1963, institutional investors owned 26 per cent of the ordinary shares of listed companies. This rose to 37 per cent in 1969, 40 per cent in 1970 and 52 per cent by 1975.[18] The norm was never to hold more than five per cent of the equity in any one firm, largely to reduce any risk of undue exposure from concentrating equity ownership in a limited number of companies. Despite the growth in equity holdings, the influence of institutional investors of UK paled in comparison with those in Germany and Japan where large block holdings (especially by banks) together with two-tier board systems mean large shareholders exist with sufficient equity holdings to influence the company.[19]

II

The theoretical literature can tend to operate in a political vacuum in which the implications of the political climate on the behaviour of shareholders is ignored.[20] Yet the prevailing political mood could be crucial. Three areas of public policy are pertinent in this respect. They all relate to the official stance on intervention in the markets: does Government intervene if, and when, markets are seen to fail, or should Government leave perceived failures for the markets to rectify? An interventionist Government in the UK typically has pursued one or more of three policy stances in relation to industry: public ownership, regulation and the promotion of mergers and take-overs. All will have implications on how managers and owners behave. But all will also have wider and specific implications for corporate governance.

Nationalisation, both actual and perceived, will influence the behaviour of both industry and the 'City'. Public ownership in the UK was not restricted to industry. At times, the public ownership of leading financial institutions was seriously mooted in the Labour Party. Real or threatened nationalisation would affect the 'City' insofar as the leading institutions would wish to ensure such action was not translated into reality and, as such, be loathe to undertake any action which might bring adverse attention to themselves. Thus, for example, forcing a major company (especially when that company was a major employer) into liquidation could have adverse consequences for the 'City' institutions. Real or threatened nationalisation of an industrial company would influence both shareholders and managers: for the latter, public ownership removed the threat of liquidation and, as such, a credible threat. Shareholders, meanwhile, could well view the possibility of public ownership as abrogating them of their ownership responsibilities. Government, moreover, may offer existing shareholders a better price than the 'market' and, as such, a way for shareholders to protect their asset values. Periods when public ownership was a possibility could act therefore to alleviate both shareholders and managers from their ownership and managerial responsibilities respectively. And the more public ownership was a possibility, the more shareholders and managers could avoid fulfilling such responsibilities, and the more likely public ownership became.

The problems of BLMC coincided with a period of time when public ownership of both financial institutions and industrial companies was a real possibility.[21] The issue of public ownership applied not only to the 'under-performing' company. In the late 1960s and through the 1970s, the agenda included firms in strategic sectors, identified as being crucial to the long-term health of the economy. This anticipation was at its height in the early and mid 1970s. Such was the mood in certain sections of the Labour Party that the 1971 Conference passed resolutions advocating the nationalisation of all banking and insurance companies.[22] The movement reached its apogee in 1973, when influential voices in the Labour Party called for the nationalisation of twenty-five of the country's top one hundred companies. The reasoning behind such moves was to influence all key sectors of the economy. If government owned the largest firm in each sector, it could set an agenda on profit performance, dividend payout, industrial relations, and so on. Other firms would be forced to follow suit.[23]

Public ownership was not limited to debates in Labour Party circles. In 1971, the Heath Government had intervened to bring Rolls Royce into public ownership. Events at that company were characterised by an absence of 'voice' by financial institutions and an assumption that Government would bail those companies out and assume ownership responsibilities.[24] When Government fulfilled such expectations, the lessons for both owners and managers was clear: public ownership was a real possibility from a Conservative Government: owners could be relieved of their ownership responsibilities and managers did not have to fear liquidation. If skewed ownership acted to deter active exercise of ownership responsibilities, interventionist public policy regimes which offered the 'promise' of public ownership made owners even less likely to intervene.

The second strand of public policy which influenced behaviour was that of take-overs and mergers.[25] 'City'-industry relations and the operation of the external mechanisms of corporate governance have rarely in the UK been dominated by either the full exit or the voice strategy. If the structure of share ownership prompted the former over the latter, public policy regimes have influenced and encouraged a propensity for limited exit and the latent tendency of shareholders to treat equity as conferring property rights, which may be transferred to the highest bidder, rather than as conferring ownership responsibilities. Limited exit has always been the key option. In this scenario, the principal sells sufficient shares to effect a fall in the market price which makes the company vulnerable to take-over. This gives warning to management that unless performance is improved, they are at risk of take-over.

Take-over presumes the credibility of the threat that another company might wish to launch a take-over bid and the existence of a public policy regime which welcomes take-over. For the former to operate, there must be agents willing and able to prompt and effect take-over; for the latter to function, public policy has to stress the benefits of take-over against the costs of potential monopoly if and when mergers and take-overs occur. At various points of time in the twentieth century Government has favoured take-over as a mechanism for restoring the fortunes of industry: as in the 1930s and again in the 1960s and 1980s. In the 1960s, the emphasis was on 'big is beautiful' and the benefits which would follow if and when large firms emerged capable of recouping economies of scale which would, it was believed, enable them better to cope in the global market place.[26] Such was the faith in such policies in the late 1960s, that a special Government agency, the Industrial Reorganisation Corporation, was established to encourage mergers and take-overs – and such was the zeal for such policy within that agency that it intervened in the market to ensure the successful take-overs by its favoured candidates of given companies.[27]

By the early 1970s, the merger zeal of the 1960s had waned. Its repercussions remained. First, the limited success (in terms of the performance of the newly merged firms) had dampened enthusiasm for such activities. Second, it had warned the major financial institutions that their views counted for nothing, if Government decided to back a given company. GEC's take-over of AEI and George Kent's takeover of Cambridge Instruments took place against the wishes of the major financial institutions: the latter was forced through as a result of the IRC actively intervening in the markets to aquire sufficient shares to ensure its success.[28]

Public policy regimes which favoured the encouragement of take-over also brought in their wake tensions between Government, the 'City' and industry as Government found its policies at the mercy of financiers who from the mid 1960s took advantage of the policy regimes to instigate take-over bids backed by international finance and facilitated by the share trading activities of the nominee, unit and investment trust funds. Lohnro, Goldsmith and Slater prompted frenzied share trading in target companies. Their activities underlined the sense in which the 'old' and 'comfortable' arms-length relations between 'City' and industry could be overruled and replaced by aggressive take-over activity made possible by the trading of the 'new' financial institutions with access to international flows of finance. 'Old' institutions may have pleaded (with good reason) to an absence of 'short termism'; the 'new' institutions felt no such loyalty. The arrival of the 'new' aggressive short termist financial institutions and the rise of the asset stripping risk-taking financial entrepreneurs added an additional and powerful constraint on any latent tendency on the part of other financial institutions to exercise 'voice'.[29]

The influence of public policy on corporate governance in the UK, therefore, has been either to prompt the exercise of limited exit (take-over eras) or to dissuade certain institutions from exit or limited exit (public ownership eras). The emphasis has never been on the exercise of the voice option. To that extent public policy has reinforced the incentives to stress ownership rights rather than responsibilities and to reinforce the disincentives to the exercise of ownership responsibilities. As the above paragraphs indicate, prevailing public policy regimes have to be included in any analysis of corporate governance and, in particular, on the behaviour of both managers and owners.

III

The way in which the strategies of the key interested parties and eventual outcomes may be determined is best modelled in terms of game-theory, in which the alternate strategies that each player (for example, the principal) will be influenced by assumptions about the other player's (the agent's) behaviour. Thus, bargaining positions and moves will be influenced by how each 'player in the game' believes the other 'player' will act. In its most simple terms, the model assumes one-off games involving two players, starting from a beginning position and considering their best moves; the more sophisticated versions assume repeated games with more than one player. The players do not need to know *exactly* what the other player will do; they do need, however, to consider the implications of any move made by other player on their own position. We can now apply this approach to the positions of key protagonists at BLMC.

In this section we consider two questions: first, who were the key protagonists and what was the nature of their stakes in the company; second, what strategies were available to them. In order to answer both questions, we have used the company's share registers which list, by named individual and institution, the number of shares held, the number of shares transacted and the date of the transaction for each year. The start position is 1970: two years after the merger between BMC and Leyland which created BLMC; a year in which profits had slumped, dividends had fallen by nearly 75 per cent as exports collapsed and the home market slumped.

For BLMC, we identify four key protagonists: institutional shareholders, a charitable trust, the banks[30] and Government (Figure 4.1). Institutional shareholders may be divided into those with small and those with large equity stakes in BLMC. The insurance companies are easily identified as holding and being responsible for specific accounts in BLMC and fell into two quite distinct groups: those with large and those with small holdings.[31] Banks fulfilled two roles in relation to the company: that of providers of working capital and administrators of equity portfolio.[32] Government, whilst not being a shareholder, was a major stakeholder.[33]

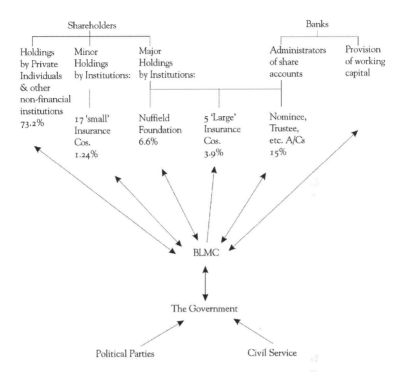

Figure 4.1 The Players in the BLMC Game in 1969

Key:

Percentage figures relate to the share of the company's total nominal share capital (600 million) in 1969.

Banks are represented as providers of working and loan capital for the company, and in their capacity as administrators and trustees of equity accounts in the company.

Shareholders are divided into financial institutions with small amounts of equity and those with large amount (more than 1 per cent) of the share capital of BLMC.

The Government is composed of political parties concerned about the employment implications of the company's problems and the civil service who shared this concern and who took over responsibility for the administration of the Industrial Reorganisation Corporation's loan.

There are, in theory, four possible moves open to shareholders: do nothing (neutral), sell all their shares (dump), sell some of their shares (drip) or exercise the voice option (voice). Of the four courses of action, voice is least likely since no one institution had sufficient shares to influence the company. Dump is the most likely assuming that all institutions seek to protect and maximise their portfolios. Drip is possible but contains a risk of being left with marked down shares on portfolios; as would any 'neutral' strategy. One would therefore expect concerns about the medium and long run viability of the company to precipitate selling by shareholders anxious to protect their future income streams. Each player, however, had to consider the implications of any move it made on the behaviour of others.

The strategies and actions of the major players were built around perceptions of how their individual actions would impact on the behaviour of others. None of the above parties could determine strategy in isolation: all had to take into consideration, when determining their strategy, how they believed others would act and how such action would impact on share prices. The positions and moves by each of the players depended upon their 'guesses' of how each other would behave. In this respect, the position of the Nuffield Foundation as a major shareholder and that of the Government as a major stakeholder were crucial. In 1969, the majority shareholder was the Nuffield Foundation which held 39.6 million shares (6.6 per cent of the total nominal share capital) with a market value of £24.7 million in BLMC.[34] The Nuffield Foundation alone held more shares in BLMC than all the insurance companies put together in 1969. The Foundation had particular cause for concern because it relied almost exclusively on income from its BLMC shares to fund its charitable activities. BLMC equity accounted for ninety-three per cent of the Foundation's assets; the dividend income from the shares represented sixty-five per cent of its income.[35] The Foundation's room for manoeuvre in the event of under-performance and hence threat to dividend income, however, was constrained. The Foundation's equity holding was bequeathed to it by the founder of Morris Motors, Lord Nuffield and the terms of the Nuffield Foundation deeds precluded sales.[36] For management the message was clear: its majority shareholder could not express exit; for other major institutional shareholders the message was equally clear that their influence could always be over-ruled by that of the Foundation: this made an exit strategy more rather than less likely in the event of under-performance.

How and why the government emerged as a key player in the game is an essential part of the BLMC game.[37] It is now a truism that BMC was dominated by a 'production ethos', by which is meant that managerial strategy was rooted in the belief that all the company had to do was to make cars. From the 1950s, the company saw and presented itself as a national institution which no Government would allow to fail. Such a view was encouraged when the Government played an active part, through the Industrial Reorganisation Corporation, in the 1968 merger.[38] Former civil servants associated with the company from the late 1960s until the mid 1980s, politicians and the company's former management all agree that BLMC's role as major employer and exporter gave the company enormous leverage with government and 'the City'.[39] Whilst management believed its major shareholder could not exit and that government would protect the company as a major employer and exporter, there was no real incentive to change. Shareholders meanwhile would feel additional reason not to exert voice.

Possible moves and outcomes by the principal protagonists are set out in Figure 4.2. Small institutions (Line 1) refers to financial institutions with only small holdings. Within this group we include the many accounts administered by the banks. They held insufficient shares to express voice (Box 4, lines 1 and 2). Their best and most likely move in the face of sustained under-performance by the company was to exit at a high price. One would therefore expect to find such shareholders adopting a full exit strategy. This, however, would create problems for the other interested parties. If only a few *individual* small institutions 'dumped' or 'dripped' shares, it would have little effect on the market price (Boxes 1 and 2; lines 1 and 2, the price would stay high). If, however, a large number of the small institutions decided to exit and *together* sold large numbers of shares, the market price would, especially if this prompted 'panic' selling on the part of the large number of private shareholders, fall (Boxes 1 and 2, lines 1 and 2, the price would fall to low).[40] Small scale selling would have no impact (the price would remain high); large scale selling could drive down the market price, especially if this precipitated selling by private and other non-financial institutions (the price would be low).

The behaviour of the smaller institutions and private shareholders had implications for the larger institutions: they could find themselves with marked down shares on their portfolios. This situation would create a potential worst case scenario for the larger institutions – of the smaller insurance companies and the banks setting the pace by engaging in large scale selling. The optimal strategy for them was to exit discreetly at a high price. But given the shares they held, it would be difficult for them to exit without anyone noticing. The signals sent by the major institutional holders would be assigned greater weight than that of smaller holders and they 'could not sell without turning the market against them.'[41] The large shareholders had to be aware of the behaviour of other institutions

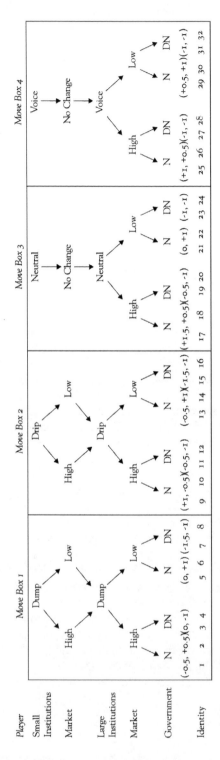

Figure 4.2 Decision Tree of 'The BLMC Game': Shareholders, The Market and The Government

Key

Large Institution – shareholders with large number of BLMC shares Small Institutions – shareholders with small number of BLMC shares Dump – sell all shares and exit the company

Drip – sell some shares in the company

Neutral – sell no shares (do nothing)

Voice – attempt to influence through meetings, etc. High/Low – high/low market price

N – Government nationalises BLMC

DN – Government does not nationalise BLMC (. . . . . .) – Large Institution, Government

(+/-) – + = 'gain' – = 'lose'

(-1, +1) – represents the maximum and minimum positions, with +1.5 being the best outcome, -1.5 being the worst outcome over which they had no control and whose actions could drive down the market price. Therefore, for the large insurance shareholders the worst case scenarios are represented by the entries for Identities 7 and 15, where small institutions set the pace, the government failed to buy out the remaining equity and the large institutions were left with marked down shares on their portfolios.

Although, *in theory*, institutions with large shareholdings could exert voice (Box 4) this was unlikely. A voice move was not attractive given the shares they held, the time and energy and hence 'free-rider' issues expended in that action and was always going to be problematic whilst the Nuffield Foundation remained the major shareholder. In addition, there was the major disincentive of no guarantee that the price would stay high. Neutrality was unlikely since that would leave their investments exposed. Discreet selling by a 'drip' policy was attractive when seen in isolation but ran the serious risk of driving down the market price in a repeated game with the smaller institutions. No one wanted a dump move which would have provoked liquidation. For the large institutions the best case scenario were Identities 9 and 17 where the Government buys out all their shares at a high price. Nationalising at a low price (Identities 5, 13, 21 and 29) was better than not nationalising at a low price. The Government, meanwhile, had the option of nationalising or not nationalising; if it opted for the former the preference would be to buy up remaining shares at a low (All boxes, lines 4 and 5 where the Government nationalises at a low price) rather than a high price. The worst case scenario for the Government was Identity 4 where shares were dumped at a high price and nationalisation did not take place: the company is effectively liquidated and massive employment losses follow.

We have then a situation where the majority of shares were distributed amongst a large number of private and small financial institutional shareholders who could, if they chose to sell, drive down the market price. Banks had a large presence, but had limited control over the shares they administered, whilst insurance companies were split between those with small and those with large shareholdings in the company. The Prudential had large holdings, and a history of intervention both in this and other companies, but its holdings were dwarfed by the Nuffield Foundation which could not sell its shares. In the meantime, the government, whilst not a shareholder, was a key interested outside party anxious to protect the employment implications of any difficulties the company experienced. How the game worked out in practice, and as the company's performance deteriorated, is discussed in Section IV below.

IV

In this section we use data from the share price registers to identify the behaviour (sell, buy, do nothing) of the shareholders of BLMC between 1970 and 1975 and complement this with other, qualitative, primary source archives and original interviews to identify evidence of 'voice' by the shareholders and by Government. In terms of the latter we separate the actions of politicians from those of civil servants.

There are several surprises from the analysis of BLMC's share-registers which run counter to the conventional view of widescale dumping in the face of company under-performance. The first is the absence of *any* selling by the major insurance shareholders. The second, as Table 4.2 indicates, is the fact that they actually *increased* their holdings.[42] The third is that voice was pursued by these institutions. The fourth is the reduction in the holdings of the Nuffield Foundation which indicates that, despite the terms of their deeds, exit could and did occur. A predictable finding is that the small financial institutional shareholders did exit the company and that it was their behaviour which determined market prices.

Sections II and III hypothesised that insurance companies with small holdings would exit because their holdings were not sufficient to drive down the market price and exit constituted no real risk for them. This is indeed what happened (Table 4.2). The smaller insurance companies adopted both exit and limited exit strategies. Four expressed full exit (Provident Mutual in 1969; Scottish Union and National Provident in 1970; London Assurance in 1974); nine actively traded shares in the company (Eagle Star in 1974; Equitable Life in 1971 and 1973; Equity and Law in 1974; London Assurance in 1970, 1972 and 1973, London Life in 1974; London and Manchester in 1972; Provident Life in 1969; Royal Insurance in 1971, 1973 and 1974; Scottish Mutual in 1972).[43]

The major Banks were equally prone to exit. Lloyds closed down accounts holding 1,337,500 shares and cut the number of shares it managed from just over 17 million in 1973 to nearly 14.5 million at April 1974. Barclays traded nearly a million shares but still overall managed holdings of 50.4 million at April 1974. Nearly half a million shares were wiped off the Midland's managed accounts in the year ending April 1974, leaving the Bank with nearly 36 million shares under its management.[44] Given that most of this trading derived from nominee accounts, the Banks themselves cannot be said to have precipitated any crisis in their role as managers of equity portfolios. The combined behaviour of the smaller financial institutions and the Banks, however, was bad news for

Table 4.2 Shareholdings in British Leyland Motor Corporation by Insurance Companies, year-ending (number of ordinary shares) 1968–1974

	1968	1969	1970	1971	1972	1973	1974
Co-Op	5414645	5414645	5414645	5664645	5664645	6150285	6150285
Eagle Star	737436	737436	2130430	2650722	2911457	3076497	2413881
Equitable Life	0	205000	205000	200000	205000	200000	200000
Equity & Law	682500	1037500	2000000	2000000	2150000	2545000	2121000
London Assurance	225175	382485	137260	1203860	1176360	634312	0
London Life	92063	203000	17963	283999	285249	535249	532318
London & Manchester	6926	1290	6548	2016513	876730	1781240	2015375
National Provident	121799	145000	0	350000	0	0	0
Norwich Union	1029525	1184250	381000	2876650	3126650	3775687	3775687
Pearl Assurance	803576	1507015	2311091	2311091	2311091	2715791	2715791
Provident Life	51350	23800	75150	75150	75150	155384	255384
Provident Mutual	400000	0	0	0	0	0	0
Prudential	12518345	11945459	27155173	28148123	28712223	30065656	30069657
Royal Exchange	146310	180750	905000	765000	955000	345000	163400
Royal Insurance	724630	1114685	1839315	2442105	3489576	3936251	3985451
Royal London Mutual	1613626	3403732	5017358	5017358	5017358	5078533	5078533
Scottish Amicable	25000	106250	600000	600000	781106	820822	1120822
Scottish Mutual Assurance	378800	480000	700000	700000	500000	500000	800000
Scottish Provident	220000	671200	1050000	1061850	1061850	1500000	1500000
Scottish Union	140000	300000	0	0	0	0	0

(Continued)

Table 4.2 (Continued)

	1968	1969	1970	1971	1972	1973	1974
Scottish Widows	700343	1159375	1859718	1859718	1859718	1859718	1859718
United Friendly	341797	683082	1024879	1024879	1031829	1152044	1152044
Total	26373846	30885954	52830530	61251663	62190992	66827469	65909346
Total Nominal Share Capital of BL	6 million	6 million	6 million	6 million	7 million	7 million	7 million
Share of above institutions	4.40	5–15	8.81	10.21	8.88	9–55	9.42
Share of top three	3.26	3.46	6.26	6.47	5–63	5–90	5–90

Source: British Leyland Motor Corporation, Annual Register of Shareholdings, Companies House, London.

the insurance companies with large shareholdings; the market was driving the price down – their worst case scenario.

The conventional literature would predict that the behaviour of the banks, the smaller financial institutions and the failure of the 'carrot' mechanism would all *add* to the incentives for the other major institutions to exercise the exit option: either discreetly or by dumping their shares on the market. The evidence from the share registers is clear: they did neither (Table 4.2). Contrary to the conventional view of arms-length relationships and of a propensity to exit behaviour, the major institutions demonstrated loyalty, in terms of holding and even *increasing* their equity holdings.[45] By 1974, the share of the 'Big Five' insurance companies had risen to just over seven per cent of the company's total nominal share capital.[46] Out of choice, the Prudential increased the size of its holdings. The shares held by the Prudential by 1975 gave it a far greater influence on BL than any of the top five institutional voting blocs had in General Motors in 1992 and put it on a par with the influence of the Sakura, Sanwa and Tokai Banks in Toyota in 1992.[47]

The Nuffield Foundation meanwhile found itself in a difficult position. Much of its income derived from the returns it made on its equity holdings in the company: if it was to fulfil its objectives, it had to protect that income. The terms of its trust deeds, however, forbade sales of that equity unless under exceptional circumstances. If Nuffield were to sell, that in turn would send signals to the market and could precipitate a crisis of confidence in the company. This created real pressures for the Foundation as the market was particularly aware of and sensitive to whether the Foundation would sell some if not all of its BLMC stock.[48] How could the Foundation protect its income, meet the conditions of the trust deeds and not prompt widespread sales in BLMC shares?

Once dividends were seriously threatened the loyalty of the Foundation was put to the test. That loyalty proved to be short-lived. In 1970 the Foundation took the decision to reduce its reliance on BLMC shares; by the spring of 1975 it had disposed of nearly a third of its BLMC shares (a reduction from nearly 40 million at the end of the 1960s to just over 25 million by April 1975).[49] The manner in which the Foundation reduced its exposure on its BLMC portfolio, whilst not precipitating widespread panic selling was to engineer a switch of its equity to the company itself in the form of a management share incentive scheme. This meant it avoided dumping large numbers of BLMC shares on the market.[50] But BLMC's share scheme failed to align managerial with shareholder interests; largely because of management's own apparent lack of enthusiasm.[51]

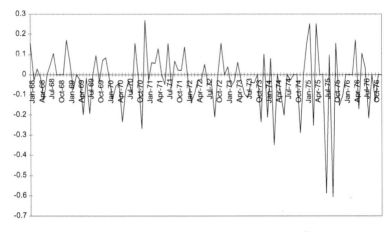

Figure 4.3 BLMC Dividend Returns

Source: The London Business School, London Share Price Database and Bespoke Data Service, Company Code File Ref 802.

Our third surprise, found by consultation of the contemporary press, was that of evidence of 'voice' by the major financial institutions. By the autumn of 1970, there were serious concerns in the 'City' about the performance of BLMC. This followed nine months of increasing evidence of financial problems in the company.[52] Of more immediate concern to shareholders were returns which, throughout 1970, were negative and, after a brief rally in August, plunged to an historic low (Figure 4.3). Major shareholders began to explore *ad hoc* joint action.[53] There were rumours that the key institutions were increasingly unhappy about the company and were calling for changes in top management. Movements to impose change derived from joint rather than sole meetings and soundings. The aim was not to persuade existing management to change, but to replace Stokes by a trio of General Motors executives.[54] This would not have been the first time the Prudential had actively involved itself in action to change management, nor the only time the institutions had joined together to press for managerial change.[55] In this instance the action changed nothing. Despite the evident dissatisfaction and attempts to change management, this came to nothing. Stokes was not removed and no major strategic changes followed at the company.

Why was there *any* attempt to exercise the voice option in BLMC? 'City' involvement in the company, and hence some obligation to intervene, derived from three sources. Many City institutions were large share-holders in the company and thus had an incentive to protect their assets. There was also the question of reputation and previous attempts at reform through take-over at stake. The City and the Industrial Reorganisation Corporation had engineered the 1968 merger between BMC and Leyland which created BLMC and thereby might be deemed responsible in part for the fortunes of the resultant company.[56] Large amounts of money had been lent to the company in support of the merger. By September 1970, outstanding loans from the Industrial Reorganisation Corporation stood at £30m.[57] The Prudential, and other institutions, had committed capital assets to a reformed company by agreeing to take-over.

Neither of the above considerations by themselves would be sufficient to prompt action. Both are causal factors in interventionist activities. The catalyst was a general anticipation that the company would soon need fresh capital, despite the fact that in 1970 the company had bank loans, overdrafts and other short term loans totalling £145.7m (an increase of about £32m on the previous year), of which nearly 90 per cent was unse-cured, as well as loan capital and long term loans totalling £81.9m.[58] The fixed assets of the company at this time were valued at £184m and post-tax profits had slumped in the year by over £18m.[59] The prospect of fur-ther capital injection cannot have been welcome news for the 'City'. The 'City' was both an unwilling principal and a provider of capital. Being asked to provide risk capital for an under-performing company (and fac-ing political opprobrium if it refused) might be expected to concentrate the mind.

It might be predicted that the failure of these behind closed doors attempts to reverse under-performance would make the institutions more likely to exit the company. Yet, as the registers make clear, the major shareholders stayed loyal and even increased their holdings. Why? BLMC's major insurance shareholders found themselves in a 'lock-in' position. We suggest several reasons for this. Limited exit to effect a fall in the market price which made the company vulnerable to take-over was not a viable strategy: by this time there was no credible threat of any other company wishing to take BLMC over. Given the size of their equity holdings, major institutional shareholders would not want to see any sustained and/or substantive decline in the value of their shares.[60] A capital asset appreciation policy would require that the value of their holdings be maintained and would deter sales which might pre-cipitate wider share selling. Small scale selling would be insufficient to reduce the exposure; wide scale selling could be sufficient to cause the price to fall substantially. A profit maximising strategy could easily be transferred into a strategy in which the viable option was to look to minimise potential loss.

But the crucial explanation is rooted in the political atmosphere. The possibility of nationalisation of BLMC (Figure 4.2) offered the 'City' a way out. If the Government were to buy out the BLMC shares, then the principals would protect their financial interests. The prospect of Government rescue created a new strategic scenario. Government intervention might release them from the contractual costs of intervention and, in addition, might also open up an asset protection option. If the Government were to buy out their shares, this would minimise loss. The risk, of course, was what price the Government would pay. On this, the principals bargained that they would get a better price from the Government than the market, and that they should hold out until they were able to sell to the former.

It is in this sense that the public policy regime was crucial in any explanation of shareholder behaviour. The analysis of corporate governance as it evolved at BLMC, however, has identified important 'surprises'. The first is that real attempt to implement internal mechanisms were applied: not via the board of the company but by the active monitoring of informed civil servants. The second is that the 'game' of transferring ownership from shareholders to the state involved a bargaining game between on the one side, the Treasury, and on the other side the Department of Trade and Industry and the shareholders.

The standard view on the internal mechanisms of corporate governance in this country is that they fail because non-executive directors have limited powers and high incentives not to press the executive directors for change. Internal mechanisms are thus seen as being so weak as to be non-existent. Whilst it is true that BLMC fulfilled all expectations of this literature, an important finding from a series of original interviews conducted with key protagonists for this paper, is that a monitoring role was undertaken, not by non-executive directors but by civil servants. From 1970, there were regular meetings between the Company and officials from the Department of Trade and Industry (hereinafter DTI), at first on a quarterly, then on a monthly basis.[61] The impetus for DTI involvement derived from two sources. The first was its on-going interests and concerns with the balance of payments implications of the company's deteriorating export performance, as well as the employment implications of the problems of British industry.[62] The second derived from its assumption of the former duties of the Industrial Reorganisation Corporation. In 1971 the winding up of the IRC transferred responsibility for the administration of the original IRC loan to the DTI.[63]

From this time on, the DTI effectively assumed the role of principal and fulfilled, in part, the external mechanisms of corporate governance which the 'City' had been unwilling or unable to do. From the company's point of view, this was the first time in its history that it had been subjected to rigorous review.[64] Regular meetings took place between the senior civil servant, four of his senior staff and two assistant secretaries from the DTI with the company's finance director and three directors. The meetings centred around the company's investment programme, the model policy and the financial results.[65] The meetings were uncomfortable. The DTI took more interest than either the banks or shareholders, subjected the company to regular meetings at which 'penetrating' questions were asked, answers demanded and outspoken comments were made about the company's inadequacies.[66]

But the DTI also faced constraints. Its leverage was its interests in employment protection and the balance of payments. Meetings were directed to questions on the company's output performance and predictions. Requests for and analyses of financial information were not raised. The DTI maintained the position that it could not intervene on such matters unless and until it became financially involved in the company: this despite its responsibility for administration of the IRC loan.[67] The DTI also realised its position was weak; it was basically reduced to trying to find out if it could salvage what was salvageable.[68] Management knew that the DTI was worried about the employment consequences of any collapse; the DTI knew that management knew. And in the meantime, shareholders knew that the civil service were concerned and moves to take the company into public ownership were strong in certain political quarters.

All parties, namely the official 'City' principals and the unofficial 'DTI' principals adopted hands-off satisficing strategies, waiting for the inevitable crisis to occur. The 'City' principals self evidently decided they would not be the ones to act as catalyst. In the current political climate, and given the expectation that, if the worst came to the worst, the government would buy out their shares, there was little incentive for them to do otherwise. The expectation that rescue would come in the form of Government aid was reinforced with the election of the Labour Government in 1974. From that time, the Government was actively seeing rescue of the company as falling within its remit and the company actively seeking Government help as the 'City' refused to bail it out. 'An ambulance for failed firms' was how Benn described extension of public ownership to British Leyland.[69] In the meantime, managers felt under no real threat from anyone, and workers knew that whatever happened, the company would not be allowed to go under.

The Government stood back, caught between the Treasury which did not want to pay a high price and the DTI which wanted to intervene immediately. The question was not if but when nationalisation would occur and the price at which the Government would buy. It became a cat and mouse game. The stakes were the price at which the government would buy out the shares. By 15 November 1974 Stokes was approaching Benn with a direct request that the Government buy out the equity.[70] But it was the refusal by the banks to extend any more capital to BLMC in the first week of December 1974 which constituted the crisis when the stark choice was between state rescue or receivership.[71] It was the catalyst that both the official and the unofficial principals had been waiting for.[72] The banks refused more cash and received backing from the 'City' shareholders. By early December 1974 Stokes claimed that the company's shareholders were threatening to force liquidation.[73] At this time the company's share price had fallen from a high of 21.75p in 1974 to 7p, with a yield of 31.3 per cent.[74] The insurance companies had obviously decided to play a final move to try and force the Government's hand before the price collapsed further. The combination was powerful.

Negotiations proceeded.[75] The principals had played a waiting game, anticipating that they would get a better price from Government than from the market. But the longer the game went on, the more this bargaining strategy seemed threatened. As discussions ensued, the share price continued to fall. The Stock Exchange refused to stop BLMC share trading unless and until explicitly instructed to do so by the Government. The DTI pressed the Treasury, but the Treasury refused.[76] By the end of January 1975, the price had fallen to 6p with a yield of 12.4 per cent.[77] A month later, the insurance companies had formed an 'investment protection committee' comprising the Prudential and other major institutional shareholders to try to protect their interests.[78] But the Government held out for another two months, on Treasury instructions.

Share trading was eventually suspended in the third week of April 1975, by which time the share value had slumped to 6.25p (from 14.75p a year earlier) with a yield of 12.3 per cent, as shares from the numerous accounts administered by the banks were traded.[79] The guessing game played by the remaining principals appeared to be working against them. For the major shareholders the eventual deal was above the market price. Shareholders sold out to the government – at a price of 10p a share, a deal put to the company's board on 23 April 1975 as a '10p offer to put up or pull out'.[80] The Board had little option but to accept.[81] Had they sold out a year previously, they would have got a better price. But they still got a better price than the current value. By waiting, the Government was able to buy out the shares at a lower price. For the Government this meant £200 million capital equity and a 99.8 per cent share of the equity of the renamed company British Leyland Limited.[82] Early the following year 95.1 per cent of the company was transferred to the National Enterprise Board by the government.[83]

A take-over had been instigated, corporate governance had engineered a transfer of ownership and the 'City' had protected its interests through a loss minimising strategy which obviated it from responsibility for direct intervention. Nationalisation of the insurance industry did not take place. The game had been played out as a guessing and waiting game between Government and the 'City' principals, with the latter adopting a strategy of believing the Government would offer a better price than the market. In April 1975 the Government did offer a better price than the market; but a much reduced price than that of a year previously.

VI

Our case study of BLMC confirms that no one institution can determine the market price. For BLMC, it was the combined activities of the 'small' insurance companies, private individuals and, most importantly, the banks which were instrumental in this respect. Volatility and hence 'short termism' derived from these sources. It was the banks and the smaller shareholders which set the pace, not the larger institutions. There was 'short termist' exit behaviour, but not all 'City' institutions can be accused of adopting such strategy. In terms of exit and voice, the fact that the larger institutional shareholders did not sell shares and tried to exercise voice in 1970 is only surprising if one pursues a conventional and steretypical view of arms-length relations and ignores both the evidence of prior interventions by the Prudential and the subsequent findings of Gaved and Charkham.

This research suggests that the political climate in which these events took place is crucial to understanding how and why the large institutions behaved as they did. Worries about state regulation, concerns that the smaller shareholder would sell and drive down the price, and a gamble on the price the Government would pay explain why the larger institutions acted as they did. Market mechanisms may cease to function effectively if key players in the game are constrained by perceptions of public policy intervention.

In practice, the insights offered in the theoretical and recent empirical literatures on corporate governance provide a powerful tool for the analysis of relations between 'City' and industry in the historical past. But empirical analysis based on case study from the historical past also has much to offer the contemporary corporate governance literatures. The evidence in relation to BLMC foresees contemporary trends: large shareholders are loyal, for reasons of lock-in, rather than loyalty to the company, whilst volatility derives from the smaller shareholders. Aggregate analysis disguises a bipartite shareholding structure and hence different behaviour patterns by financial shareholders. The firm is under some short term pressure, volatility does exist, but it derives from the smaller shareholders who, given the size of their holdings, exert no real pressure over management. Diffuse small holdings by numerous bodies or institutions can act as a constraint upon change. Voice was self-evidently unsuccessful.

Our analysis of the history of BLMC's relations with its shareholders adds substance to the Mayer thesis that major shareholders can find themselves in a 'lock-in' position and may, as a result of the disincentives to intervene, opt for merger as a mechanism for replacing underperforming management. Conyon's thesis that contemporary share incentive schemes fail to realign managerial with shareholder interests and that ill-defined incentive structures for non-executive directors may constrain effective corporate governance mechanisms finds support from our analysis. A key finding is that the key movers were neither the insurance companies with large shareholdings nor the Government. The banks and those insurance companies with small holdings set the pace. It was their actions which collectively drove the market price down and forced the outcome. This suggests the need for a move away from seeing the banks only in a capital providing role towards an exploration of their influence on the equity markets.

The analysis underlines the importance of greater awareness of the political environment when examining the 'short termist' equity trading behaviour of the financial institutions by warning of the risks of ignoring the political climate in which both principals and agents operate: a truism which applies to both sides of the Atlantic.[84] It equally reinforces Roe's view that the 'spectre' of nationalisation, be of industrial companies or of the financial institutions themselves has to be taken into consideration when examining the relationships between industry and the 'City' in the UK in the post-war years. Corporate governance and its implications both for 'City'-industry relations and the rectification of company underperformance can no longer be assessed in a political vacuum; prevailing public policy regimes set the framework in which actors operate. The research agenda has to incorporate explicitly the influence of public policy on corporate governance.

Did the 'City' fail British industry? This study raises serious doubts. All players were locked into a zero sum game. The only real beneficiaries were the insurance companies with small holdings who were able to exit at a high price. The research agenda must be to pursue analyses of 'City'-industry relations which tracks share transactions behaviour allowing for differential behaviour by named institutions and which explicitly incorporates into the analysis the implications of perceptions of public policy regimes on incentive structures. There is now a growing literature which acknowledges the influence of public policy on corporate governance in contemporary events as well as the recent past. The record of corporate governance at BLMC was not a one-off, a unique case. It was only unusual if a stereotypical view of 'City'-industry relations is pursued. The reality is of complex inter-linkages and bargaining structures influenced both by the relative size of share holding by City institutions and by perceptions of government policy in the UK. Corporate governance at BLMC was determined by perceptions of how Government and 'small' shareholders would behave and a guessing game between the 'City', civil servants and the Treasury. An aversion to exit on the part of the major City institutions was not the result of loyalty to the company per se but the powerful combination of fear of provoking greater state regulation of the financial institutions coupled with a belief that the Government would give them a better price than the market. In neo-classical terms, the market mechanism could not work given perceptions of potential moves by political agents. In these terms, and contrary to standard analyses, we place public policy at the centre of the analysis of City/industry relations. The premise is not to 'defend' the 'City', nor to challenge the orthodox view, but rather to tease out exactly how and why different institutions behaved in the way they did, and to draw out the lessons from this case study for the evolution of corporate governance in the UK.

Notes

* My thanks to Andrew Gamble, John Wilson, Mike Dietrich and Meghnad Desi.
1 See, for example, the work of Broadberry, Crafts and Bean on collusive practices in the inter and post-war decades; that of Elbaum and Lazonick on institutional rigidity dating back to the later Victorian years; and that of Tolliday and Zeitlin on why mass production techniques were not viable, given demand constraints, in the interwar years. (S. N. Broadberry and N. F. R. Crafts, 'Explaining Anglo-American productivity differences in the mid-twentieth century', *Oxford Bulletin of Economics and Statistics*, Vol. 52 (1990),

pp. 375–402 and 'Britain's productivity gap in the 1930s', some neglected factors', *Journal of Economic History*, Vol. 52 (1992), pp. 531–58; Bernard Elbaum and William Lazonick (eds), *The Decline of the British Economy* (Oxford: Clarendon Press, 1986); S. Tolliday and J. Zeitlin, *The Automobile Industry and its Workers: Between Fordism and Flexibility* (Cambridge, 1987).

2 The key theoretical texts are Oliver Hart, *Firms, Contracts and Financial Structure* (Oxford: Clarendon, 1995), Oliver Hart, 'Corporate governance: some theory and implications', *Economic Journal*, Vol. 105 (1995), pp. 678–689, S. J. Grossman and O. D. Hart, 'An analysis of the principal agent problem', *Econometrica* (1983), Vol. 51, pp. 7–45; and Albert O. Hirschamn, *Exit, Voice and Loyalty; Responses to Decline in Firms, Organizations and States* (Cambridge, Mass.: Harvard University Press, 1970). More empirically based work is found in Nicholas Dimsdale, 'Restoring corporate accountability' in Nicholas Dimsdale and Martha Prevezer (eds), *Capital Markets and Corporate Governance* (Oxford: Clarendon Press, 1994); Paul Marsh, *Short Termism on Trial* (London: Institutional Fund Managers Association, 1990) and Paul Marsh, 'Market assessment of company performance' in Dimsdale and Prevezer, *Capital Markets* as well as Steve Nickell, *The Performance of Companies* (Oxford: Blackwell, 1994). A good example of the 'popular' view is Will Hutton, *The State We're in* (London: Jonathan Cape, 1995) . See also the very different views of David Miles, 'Asking the right questions?' in Simon Milner (ed.), *Could Finance Do More for British Business?* (London: Institute for Public Policy, 1996), Colin Mayer, 'Stock-Markets, financial institutions and corporate performance' in Dimsdale and Prevezer (eds) *Capital Markets*, Colin Mayer, 'Corporate governance and performance: the evidence', in Andrea Westall (ed.), *Competitiveness and Corporate Governance* (London: Institute for Public Policy, 1996) and Will Hutton, 'Failings of the British financial system', in Milner (ed.) *Could Finance do more for British Business?*

3 See Mark J. Roe, *Strong Managers, Weak Owners: The Political Roots of American Corporate Finance* (Princeton: Princeton University Press, 1970).

4 Sue Bowden and Josephine Maltby, 'More a national asset than an investor's paradise; financial management and the British Motor Corporation', *Accounting, Business and Financial History*, Vol. 8, No. 2 (1998), pp. 137–164; Sue Bowden and Paul Turner, 'Uncertainty and The Competitive Decline of The British Motor Industry, 1945–1975', *New Political Economy*, Vol. 3, No. 1 (1998), pp. 103–120; Roy Church, *The Rise and Decline of the British Motor Industry* (London: Macmillan, 1994); James Foreman-Peck, Sue Bowden, and Alan McKinlay, *The British Motor Industry* (Manchester: Manchester University Press, 1995); Karel Williams, 'BMC/BLMC/BL – A misunderstood failure' in Karel Williams, John Williams, and Dennis Thomas, *Why are the British Bad at Manufacturing?* (London: Routledge and Kegan Paul, 1983).

5 Roy Church, 'Deconstructing Nuffield: The evolution of managerial culture in the British motor industry', *Economic History Review*, XLIX, 3 (1996), pp. 561–583; Timothy Whisler, *The British Motor Industry, 1945–1994: A Case Study in Industrial Decline* (New York: Oxford University Press, 1999).

6 See Sue Bowden and Andrew Gamble, *Corporate Governance in a Political Climate; 'New' Initiatives by 'Old' Labour in the UK, 1965–1969* (Sheffield: Political Economy Research Centre, 2000).

7 In 1952 the British Motor Corporation (BMC) was formed by the merger between The Austin Motor Company Limited and Morris Motors Limited. That company was renamed British Motor Holdings (BMH) following the 1966 merger of BMC and Jaguar Cars Limited. BMH was short-lived. On 8th February 1968 British Leyland Motor Corporation (BLMC) was incorporated following the merger of BMH and The Leyland Motor Corporation Limited.

   Rescue by the Government in 1975 led to a name change. From June 1975, the company was known as British Leyland Limited. On 1 July 1978 the company was renamed BL Ltd., a name which lasted until 1986.

8 For an analysis of the financial performance of BMC in relation to that of its main UK competitors between 1952 and 1968 see Bowden and Maltby 'More a national asset'.

9 Hirschamn, *Exit, Voice and Loyalty.*

10 See Marsh, *Short Termism* and 'Market assessment' and Nickell, *The Performance.*

11 Mayer, 'Stock-Markets, financial institutions and corporate performance'.

12 An option certainly favoured by the Bank of England which was to argue that if institutional shareholders were *dissatisfied*, they should (our italics) take steps to change the composition of the Board. See, Committee to Review the Functioning of the Financial Institutions, Second Stage Evidence, Volume 4: Bank of England, Written Answers, Point 2 (b), p. 180 (1978).

13 The first has to tread a careful path and avoid insider trading. A recent example of the most extreme form of voice is the recent successful moves by the Prudential and other major institutional shareholders to remove Anita Roddick from her position as CEO of The Body Shop in late spring 1998.

14 Jonathon Charkham, *Keeping Good Company* (Oxford: Claarendon, 1994); Matthew Gaved, *Closing the Communications Gap: Disclosure and Institutional Shareholders* (London: Institute of Chartered Accountants, 1997, April) and *Ownership and Influence* (London: Institute of Management, London School of Economics, 1995); G. P. Stapleton, *Institutional Shareholders and Corporate Governance* (Oxford: Clarendon, 1996).

15 Committee to Review the Functioning of Financial Institutions, Volume 5, Written Evidence by the Insurance Companies (14 November 1978), p. 65.

16 M. J. Conyon, P. Gregg, and S. Machin, 'Taking care of business; executive compensation in the UK', *Economic Journal*, Vol. 105 (1995), pp. 704–15; M. J. Conyon and D. Leech, 'Company performance and corporate governance', *Oxford Bulletin of Economics and Statistics*, Vol. 56, No. 3 (1994), pp. 229–247; M. Jensen and K. Murphy, 'Performance, pay and top management incentives', *Journal of Political Economy*, Vol. 98 (1990), pp. 225–264; M. C. Jensen, 'The modern industrial revolution: exit, and the failure of internal control mechanisms', *Journal of Finance*, Vol. XLVIII (1993), pp. 831–880; M. Jenson and W. H. Meckling, 'The Theory of the Firm: Managerial Behaviour, Agency Costs and Ownership Structure', *Journal of Financial Economics*, No. 3 (1976), pp. 305–60 and D. Yermack, 'Higher market

valuation of companies with small boards of directors', *Journal of Financial Economics*, Vol. 40 (1996), pp. 185–211.

17 The growth of the institutional investor resulted from the growing presence of pension houses and insurance companies. The growth of insurance and pensions led to a massive inflow of funds into their accounts which led to a widening and deepening of their company share portfolios. Between 1963 and 1975 the proportion of shares held by persons fell from 54 per cent to 37.5 per cent. Committee to Review the Functioning of Financial Institutions, Progress Report on the Financing of Industry and Trade, para 69, p. 20 (1977). See also, George Clayton and W. T. Osborn, *Insurance Company Investment: Principles and Policy* (London: George Allen and Unwin, 1965); W. A. Thomas, *The Finance of British Industry, 1918–1976* (London, 1978); Committee to Review the Functioning of Financial Institutions, Written Evidence by Insurance Company Associations, pp. 1–48; Committee to Review the Functioning of Financial Institutions, Progress Report, paras 69–71, pp. 20–21; Charkham, *Good Company*; Gaved, *Communications Gap*; Gaved, *Ownership and Influence*; Stapleton, *Institutional Shareholders*.

18 Committee to Review the Functioning of Financial Institutions, Evidence on the Financing of Industry and Trade, Volume 3, Written Evidence by the Stock Exchange (1978), para 14 and Chart 1, p. 9. Although internally generated funds continued to be the key source of funds for industry, the Stock Exchange was to provide an increasing source of capital. Between 1970 and 1976, stock exchange issues on average accounted for 20 per cent of additions to real fixed assets, 16 per cent by way of equity and 4 per cent by means of loan capital.

Committee to Review, Evidence from the Stock Exchange, para 27, p. 16. In 1970, it contributed £0.1 billion (as against £3.5 billion internal sources and £0.9 billion from net bank funding). By 1975, the Stock Exchange provided £1.1 billion, as against £1.8 billion from banks and £9.1 billion from internally generated funds. Committee to Review, Written Evidence by the Stock Exchange, Part II, Question No. 1, page 17, Table 2 and page 18, para 31.

19 Charkham, *Keeping Good Company*; Gaved, *Closing the Communications Gap*; Gaved, *Ownership and Influence*; Stapleton, Institutional Shareholder; Committee to Review the Functioning of Financial Institutions, Written Evidence of the Insurance Company Associations, Appendix B, paragraph 44, pp. 90–91 (April 1978).

20 Paul Marsh, 'Myths surrounding short-termism', (London: *Financial Times* 1997), Supplement: Finance, June, Part Six, pp. 6–7; Roe, *Strong Managers*.

21 Committee to Review the Functioning of Financial Institutions, Second Stage Evidence, Volume 2, Written Evidence by the Insurance Company Associations, para 43, p. 11, para 149, p. 40, para 157, p. 43.

22 Committee to Review the Functioning of Financial Institutions, Second Stage Evidence, Volume 3, Synopsis of the Written Evidence by the Committee of London Clearing Banks (November, 1977), para 113, p. 99.

23 Labour Party, Conference Report, October 1973. Tuesday morning session, pp. 170–171.

24 The collapse of Rolls Royce in 1970/1 was characterised by a singular absence of voice by any of the financial institutions. The lead, in trying to

identify and then deal with the problems of the company, was taken by the merchant banks working alongside Bank of England and Department of Trade and Industry officials. The official report did not mention this: Department of Trade and Industry, Rolls Royce Ltd and the RB 211 Aero-Engine, January 1972, Cmnd. 4860. A later, more detailed analysis did analyse in detail the role of these officials. See Department of Trade and Industry, Rolls Royce Limited, Investigation under Section 165 (a) (I) of the Companies Act 1948, Report by R. A. MacCrindle and P. Godfrey (1973), Guildhall Library Archive, London.

25 As for example those prompted by the IRC (with Government support) in the mid 1960s. These mergers were based on the premise that in order to compete internationally, Britain needed large firms run by 'modern' managers. The political strategy was to support merger as a means of achieving industrial rationalisation. For a detailed overview of the corporate governance implications of this policy regime, see Bowden and Andrew Gamble, 'Corporate Governance'. The absence of synergy in the mergers of this decade is discussed by Keith Cowling in *Monopoly Capitalism* (London: Macmillan, 1982), pp. 71–95. The mergers of the 1960s were horizontal and thus, according to Cowling, were part of the trend to monopoly capitalism. Bowden and Gamble, however, stress that the mergers were part of a wider attempt to improve corporate governance (albeit unsuccessful) which brought the Government into potential conflict with the 'City'.

26 See Leslie Hannah, *The Rise of the Corporate Economy* (London: Methuen, 1976).

27 Files Relating to the Activities of the IRC: London: Public Record Office (hereinafter PRO), EW26/60, EW26/61, EW26/69, EW27/239, EW27/291, EW27/293.

28 Merger between AEI and GEC, PRO: EW27/293; George Kent and Cambridge Instruments Merger, Papers, PRO: EW26/61 and EW26/62.

29 See Bowden and Gamble, 'Corporate Governance'.

30 There is a convention in the literature that the clearing banks were mainly concerned with the provision of working capital to British industry, but through the post-war period, with greater diversification and competition among the financial institutions, they had extended their activities to include investment management (Committee to Review, Synopsis, London Clearing Banks, Chapter 13, para. 79, p. 92 and Chapter 18, para 99, p. 96 and para. 106, p. 98; Committee to Review the Functioning of Financial Institutions, Written Evidence by the Committee of London Clearing Bankers (1977), Vol. 5, para 141, p. 158. By 1969, banks accounted for 1.7 per cent of the market value of shareholdings in UK companies (Committee to Review, Progress Report, Table 6, p. 21). This is reflected in the share registers of BLMC, where in 1973 BLMC accounts adminstered by Lloyds, The Midland, Westminster and Barclays Banks accounted for 15 per cent of the company's ordinary shares (British Leyland Motor Corporation, Annual Register of Shareholders (Companies House, London), 1973 and 1974).

31 In 1969, the five largest insurance shareholders in BLMC held just under four per cent of the total nominal share capital of BLMC. In these terms, the shareholdings of BLMC predict Gaved's and Charkham's findings for

the 1990s which identify distinct characteristics of portfolio management as between those institutions with large stakes in given companies and those who chose to spread their portfolios widely (Charkham, *Keeping Good Company*; Gaved, *Communications Gap*; Gaved, *Ownership and Influence*).

32 The existence of nominee, named, numbered and trustee accounts for each of the main banks, makes it difficult to assign responsibility and identify precise control of the shares in each account. In many instances, it may be assumed that the bank acted on behalf of and on the instruction of anonymous individuals and exercised little or no control. The shares they controlled, actively and on behalf of individuals, were nevertheless substantial.

33 Government held no shares and therefore can not at this time be viewed as a shareholder. Its interests in the company were great however: in the export earnings from motor vehicles and in the employment implications of any threatened closure of the company. Both gave Government a 'stake' in the fortunes of the company. It had also lent large amounts of money to the company in support of the 1968 merger (see page 20).

34 The Nuffield Foundation, Report for the year 1969 (Oxford:1970), Schedule 2, p. 113; Robert Jackson, *The Nuffield Story* (London: Frederick-Muller, 1964), p. 202; Adeney, *Nuffield*, p. 202; Sue Bowden and Josephine Maltby, 'Under-performance, short-termism and corporate governance; the 'City' and the British Motor Corporation, 1952–1967', *Financial History Review* (1998), pp. 179–201.

35 The Nuffield Foundation, Report 1969, Appendix II, pp. 108–109.

36 The Nuffield Foundation, Report 1969, Schedule 2, p. 113; p. 93.

37 Which will come to no surprise to those familiar with the work of Shleifer and Vishny. See Shleifer and Vishny, 'Politicians and firms', p. 995 and 'A theory of privatisation'.

38 Douglas Hague and Geoffrey Wilkinson, *The IRC – An Experiment in Industrial Intervention; A History of the Industrial Reorganisation Corporation* (London: George Allen and Unwin, 1983); G. Turner, *The Leyland Papers* (London, 1971).

39 Notes of an interview between R. Stormonth-Darling (former non-executive Director of BMC and BLMC) and G. Owen (hereinafter Stormonth interview): our thanks to Geoffrey Owen for giving us access to the transcript of this interview; Notes of interview by the author with John Barber, former Finance Director of BLMC (from 1968) and Managing Director of BLMC (until 1975), London, 27 August, 1997; DTI interview. The DTI interview refers to an interview conducted by the author on 17 October 1997 in London with one of the senior civil servants involved in these meetings. Our source wishes to remain anonymous and the confidentiality has been respected. Subsequent references thus refer to this interview as DTI interview. We are grateful to both John Barber and the annonymous civil servant for their time and help.

40 The banks, for example, had a powerful presence both as providers of working capital and as managers of equity portfolios, but their ability to fulfil any principal role in relation to the latter was constrained by the diffuse nature of their ownership and their ability to influence portfolios they managed on behalf of third parties. If the banks, either on their own initiative or on instruction, traded large numbers of the shares they administered, then the market price would fall.

41 Committee to Review, Progress Report, para 87, p. 26.

42 British Leyland Motor Corporation, Annual Register, 1968–1975.

43 British Leyland Motor Corporation, Annual Register, 1968 to 1974 inclusive.

44 British Leyland Motor Corporation, Annual Register, 1973 and 1974.

45 British Leyland Motor Corporation, Annual Register, 1968 and 1975. In addition, Royal Insurance increased its holdings over time, to join the 'large player' ranks. In 1968, this company held 0.7m shares; by 1975 it held 4m.

46 British Leyland Motor Corporation, Annual Register, 1968–1974. Five per cent is generally viewed as a significant holding and 10 per cent as constituting sufficient equity to assert a strong voice (Mayer, 'Corporate Performance', p. 189). Ten percent shares are a common phenomena in Germany where it is the norm today for three or more institutions to own 10 per cent of equity each (Rowe, *Strong Managers*, p. 172–3).

47 Rowe, Table 5, p. 173. The shares were Sakura 4.9 per cent and Sanwa 4.9 per cent. The largest three institutional voting blocs in GM were Michigan State Treasurer 1.42 per cent, Bernstein Sanford 1.28 per cent, Wells Fargo 1.20 per cent.

48 *Investors Chronicle*, 10 December 1971, p. 187

49 The Nuffield Foundation, Thirtieth Report for the Year 1975 (London, 1976), pp. 2–3.

50 It also created a 'carrot' mechanism for realigning managerial interests with those of shareholders. In the summer of 1970, an Extraordinary General Meeting of the company was called to approve the introduction of a share incentive scheme launched on the initiative of the company's finance director. The scheme was introduced by John Barber, the former Ford director who became BLMC's Finance Director in 1968. The idea was to introduce into BLMC a scheme seen to have been beneficial at Ford. Barber interview, London, 27 August, 1997. The justification was to retain and attract good management, an essential component of which strategy was 'the availability of rewards and incentives which are sufficiently competitive to counteract the attractions offered elsewhere'. The scheme offered a maximum of 14 million shares of 5s. each (about 2.5 per cent of the ordinary share capital of the company) to senior executives of the company at a subscription price not less than the official stock exchange middle market quotation on the day prior to the offer. Five per cent of the subscription price was to be payable at the time of issue and the balance payable after not less than three years. Whilst the share was partly paid it could not be transferred without the consent of the board. Non-executive directors were not eligible (British Leyland Motor Corporation, Annual Report and Accounts, 1971, p. 15).

51 Although the number of executives taking up the scheme did exceed original expectations, the number of shares each executive subscribed to signally failed to meet expectations. The original scheme estimated 150 directors for inclusion. By 1974, 181 had subscribed. The extent of under-subscription was significant, although it did improve over time. In 1971 the extent of under-subscription was just under 8 million shares. By 1974, 9.7 million of the 14 million shares had been taken up. British Leyland Motor Corporation, Annual Register, 1971–1974 inclusive.

52 The 1969 results published in January 1970 were generally viewed as 'disappointing' and by May 1970, the interim results 'were expected to be as

abysmal as they have turned out'. See, for example, adverse comment and reports on 'widespread concern' in *Investors Chronicle*, 29 May 1970, p. 1013.

53 Bowden and Maltby, 'Under-Performance'.

54 Investors Chronicle, 30 October 1973, p. 392. At the time, this would not be construed as raising questions of insider trading, because 'reputable institutions' would not trade on the basis of information available to them but not others. Committee to Review the Functioning of Financial Institutions, Second Stage Evidence, Volume 5, Written Evidence of the Department of Trade (1979), Annexe 1, para 2, p. 20.

55 In 1967, the Prudential had attempted to 'go it alone', holding weekly telephone conversations with the then managing director of BMH, George Harriman, in a 'behind closed doors' attempt to exert management change. The failure of these attempts and the free rider issues of pursuing the sole strategy persuaded the Prudential to back the merger with Leyland in 1968. This was a classic 'behind closed doors' initiative but, by taking it upon itself to approach the company in this way, the Prudential was creating its own disincentives to continue such a 'voice' strategy. Free rider considerations meant it was easier and costless for the Prudential to back the 1968 merger rather than continue efforts to persuade the company to mend its ways. See Bowden and Maltby, 'Under-Performance'.

56 Hague and Wilkinson, *The IRC*; Lewis Whyte, *One Increasing Purpose – The Annals of an Investor* (London: Hutchinson Benham, 1984).

57 British Leyland Motor Corporation Limited, Annual Report, 1971, p. 25.

58 Applies to the year ending September 1970. British Leyland Motor Corporation, Annual Report, 1971, pp. 23 and 25.

59 British Leyland Motor Corporation, Annual Report, 1971, p. 18.

60 In 1969, the Co-Op held 5.4 million shares in BLMC (worth c. £1.35m), The Prudential 11.9 million (nearly £3m), Royal Insurance 1.1 million (just over £0.25 m), Pearl 1.5 million (nearly £400,000), and Norwich Union 1.2 million (£300,000). British Leyland Motor Corporation, Annual Register, 1969. By 1973, the exposure of the Prudential and the Co-Op was in the order of £7.5m (Prudential) and £1.5m (Co-Op) (British Leyland Motor Corporation, Annual Register, 1973).

61 Barber interview; DTI interview.

62 DTI interview; Committee to Review the Functioning of Financial Institutions, Evidence on the Financing of Industry and Trade, Volume 4, Oral Evidence by the National Enterprise Board (22 November, 1977), p. 31.

63 British Leyland Motor Corporation, Annual Report, 1971, p. 14.

64 Stormonth interview; Barber interview; DTI interview.

65 DTI interview.

66 Barber interview.

67 DTI interview; Barber interview.

68 DTI interview; Barber interview.

69 Tony Benn kindly gave us access to the unedited version of his diaries. All subsequent references to the Benn diaries in this paper refer to the unedited version of the diaries. *Benn Diaries*, 6 March 1974.

70 *Benn Diaries*, 15 November 1974.

71 *The Economist*, 14 December 1974, p. 64.

72 Barber interview.
73 *Benn Diaries*, 3 December 1974.
74 *The Economist*, Weekly Share Report.
75 *The Economist*, 21 December 1974, p. 91.
76 Benn Diaries.
77 *The Economist*, Weekly Share Report.
78 *Investors Chronicle*, 7 February 1975, p. 585. See Jonathan Charkham 'Institutional Investors', p. 106.
79 *Economist*, Weekly Share Price Series, April 1974 and April 1975.
80 *Benn Diaries*, 23 April 1975; *The Economist*, 26 April, 1975, p. 88 and 21 June 1975, p. 73.
81 *Benn Diaries*, 1 May 1975.
82 *Benn Diaries*, 23 April 1975.
83 Committee to Review the Functioning of Financial Institutions, Evidence on the Financing of Industry and Trade, Volume 4, Written Evidence by the National Enterprise Board (May 1977), para 11, p. 3.
84 See, for example, A. Shleifer and R. Vishny, 'Politicians and firms', *Quarterly Journal of Economics* (1994), Vol. 109, pp. 995–1025 and 'Large shareholders and corporate control', *Journal of Political Economy*, Vol. 94, No. 3 (1986), pp. 461–488 and Harold Demsetz and Kenneth Lehn, 'The structure of corporate ownership: causes and consequences', *Journal of Political Economy*, Vol. 93, No. 6 (1985), pp. 1155–1177.

Index

Note: Numbers in italic indicate a figure and numbers in bold indicate a table on the corresponding page.

ABCC *see* Association of British Chambers of Commerce (ABCC)
advances 20–22, **36**, 72–77, 80–82
AEI 103
Anglo-South American Bank (ASAB) 15, 23, 26n55
ASAB *see* Anglo-South American Bank (ASAB)
assets 7–9, **20**, 75–76, 101–103, 115–116, 124n18
Association of British Chambers of Commerce (ABCC) 77–78, **78**, 82, **84**, 91n45

Bagehot, W. 7, 16, 59n6
Bank of England (BoE) 3, **35**, 123n12, 125n24; and limited liability banking 6, 13–16, 20, 23, 29; and small firms 71–74
Bank of Ireland **35**
Bank Rate 69, 73, 89n16, 90n43
bank regulation 2–3, 6, 12, 16, 19–20, 22–24; and corporate governance 119–121
banks: organisation of English banks before 1939 38–43, *39–40*; *see also* banks, joint-stock; banks, non-public; banks, provincial; banks, Public; commercial banks; *specific banks by name*
banks, joint-stock 9–14, **11**, *39–40*, 63n70
banks, non-public **9**

banks, provincial 9–11, **11**
banks, public 8–14, **9**, 17
Barber, John 126n39, 127n50
Barclays Bank **35**, 37, 39, 73, 110
Barings 15–17, 20, 23
big business 31, 33–35, **35**
'Big Five' 35–40, 43–46, 49–52, 54–59, 61n27, 63n65, 63–64n73
bills **36**, 40–41, *40*, 50
Birmingham Chamber of Commerce 77–78, **78**, 91n45
Black Country 74
BMC *see* British Motor Corporation (BMC)
BMH *see* British Motor Holdings (BMH)
Board of Trade 71, 85, 92n88
Board of Trade Journal 86, 92n88
BOB Ltd. 22
BoE *see* Bank of England (BoE)
Bolton Committee 71
Bowden, Sue 4, 125n25
Boyle, Sir Edward 75
branches 34–43, **36**, *40–41*, 49–56, 61n27, 63n57, 65–67
British Leyland Motor Corporation (BLMC) 4, 96–97, 101, 104–106, 110, 113–116, 118–121, 123n7, 125–126n30–31, 127n50, 128n60; decision tree of *108*; dividend returns *114*; financial performance of **97**; the players in *105*; shareholdings in **111**

British Motor Corporation (BMC) 97, 104–108, *108*, 115, 123n7–8
British Motor Holdings (BMH) 97, 123n7, 128n55
British Overseas Bank Limited 22

Cambridge Instruments 103
capital 8–9, **9**, 19–22, 30–33, 50–57; brand name capital 24n6; capital equipment 52, 76, 86; capital market 77; and corporate governance 118–120, 125n30; human capital 56; loan capital *105*, 115, 124n18; and Midland Bank expansion **36**; risk capital 82, 115; share capital 105–106, *105*, **112**, 125–126n31, 127n50; and small firms 69–70, 74–83, **78**, 86–87; working capital 74, 104, 126n40
capitalism 32, 58, 61n27, 66, 125n25
Capital Issues Committee 69
Carnevali, Francesca 3–4
Cassis, Y. 33
Census of Distribution 71
centralization 37, 43, 46–54, 63n57
Chandler, Alfred D. 3, 32–33, 56–57, 61n27
Charkham, Jonathon 119, 125–126n31
Church, Roy 96
'City,' the 4, 101–103, 107, 114–121, 125n25
City of Glasgow Bank 11, **11**, 13–14, 17
Clydesdale Bank 9–11
commercial banking industry 3, 30–38, 54–58; and corporate development and the organisation of English banks before 1939 38–43; and internal labour markets 43–46; mechanization, machine ledger keeping and centralization in 46–54; *see also* commercial banks
Commercial Bank 9–10
commercial banks 30–31, 33–35, **35**, 55–58, 65–66; and limited liability banking 15, 20–23; mechanization, machine ledger keeping and centralisation in 46–54; and small firms 71, 74, 87

corporate development 38–43, 58
corporate economy 3, 5, 30–38, 54–58; corporate development and the organisation of English banks before 1939 38–43; and internal labour markets 43–46; mechanization, machine ledger keeping and centralization in English commercial banks 46–54
corporate governance 4, 95–98, 100–104, 116–121, 125n25
Cox and Co. 21
credit restrictions 4, 70–72, 74–75, 87, 90n32, 92n90; and hire purchase 83–84, 86; and small firms 75–81, **78–79**
Crick, W. F. 37

decentralisation 39
decision tree *108*
Department of Trade and Industry (DTI) 116–118
deposits 8–9, **9**, 22, 34, 61n22; equity/deposit ratios 19–20, **19**, 28n96; and Midland Bank expansion **36**
development *see* corporate development
dividend returns 98, *114*
DTI *see* Department of Trade and Industry (DTI)

Economist, the 10
economy 69, 73–74, 81–84, 87–88, 90n32, 90n43; and corporate governance 101–102; and small firms 71–72; *see also* corporate economy
efficiency 37–38, 44, 54, 58, 71, 81
EIA *see* Engineering Industries Association (EIA)
employees 43–45; women *45*, 50, 53–54, 62n47–48; *see also* staff
Engineering Industries Association (EIA) 80–81, 91n60
equity 6–10, 15–20; average equity/deposit ratio **19**; and corporate governance 98–106, 109–110, 113–115, 118–120, 124n18, 126n40, 127n46; market value of **35**; returns on 16–18, *18*, 27n66

FBI *see* Federation of British Industry (FBI)
Federation of British Industry (FBI) 79, **79**, 91n45
firms *see* small firms
Franks, Sir Oliver 74

Gaved, Matthew 119, 125–126n31
GEC 103
governance *see* corporate governance
government 3–5, 15–16, 69–70, 72–75, 77–84, 86–87; and corporate governance 96, 101–110, *105*, *108*, 116–121, 123n7, 125n25, 126n33

Harriman, George 128n55
headquarter functions *42*
hire purchase (H.P.) 71–73, 92n84, 92n88, 92n90–91, **93–94**; and small firms 83–87, **84**
Holden, Sir Edward 37
H.P. *see* hire purchase (H.P.)

ICFC *see* Industrial Commercial & Finance Corporation (ICFC)
Industrial Commercial & Finance Corporation (ICFC) 81–83, 91n60
Industrial Reorganisation Corporation (IRC) 103, *105*, 107, 115–117, 125n25
information technology (IT) 67
IRC *see* Industrial Reorganisation Corporation (IRC)

Journal of Industrial History (*JIH*) 1–2, 5, 29, 66

Kent, George 103
Keynes, John Maynard 30, 58

labour markets 34, 37, 43–44; internal 43–46, *45*, *47–48*, *53*
Labour Party 58, 101–102
ledger keeping *see* machine ledger keeping
lender of last resort (LOLR) 13–16, 21
Levine, R. 31, 59n6
limited liability banking 3, 6; the move to 12–15; policy implications 23–24; and regulation and supervision 20–23, **20**; and stability 15–20, *18*, **19**; unlimited liability 7–12, **9**, **11**
Lloyds Bank **35**, 38–39, 73–74, 110
LOLR *see* lender of last resort (LOLR)
London and County Banking company **35**
Lothbury *42*, 50–51

machine banking *42*, 52, 67
machine ledger keeping 46–54
Macmillan Gap 4, 81–84, 87, 91n60
mechanisation 42–43, *42*, 46–55, *47–48*, *53*, 58, 63n65, 65–67
Midland Bank 35–40, **35–36**, *40*, 49–50, 61n27, 63n57, 64n78; and corporate governance 110; and small firms 73
monetary policy 2–4, 69–71, 87–88, 89n16; banking with brakes on 72–75; small firms and the British economy 71–72; small firms and the credit restrictions 75–81, **78–79**; small firms and hire purchase 83–87, **84**; small firms and the Macmillan Gap 81–83

National Provincial Bank **35**, *41*
National Union of Manufacturers (NUM) 80
Norman, Montagu 19–23
NUM *see* National Union of Manufacturers (NUM)

organisation 30–31, 33–34, 37–43, *39*, 50–51, 54–58
Oxford University: Institute of Statistics 71, 75, 83, 85–86

Parliamentary Committee of Inquiry on Small Firms *see* Bolton Committee
Parr's Bank **35**
policy *see* monetary policy
political climate 95–96, 100–101, *105*, 107, 110, 115–121, 125n25
profits 33–34, **36**, 102–104
Prudential Assurance Company Ltd. 22, 113–115, 118–119, 123n13, 128n55

public banks *see* banks, public
Public Records Office 10

Radcliffe Committee 71, 77, 79–80,
82–83
rationalisation 33, 35, 57, 61n27,
65–66, 125n25
regulation *see* bank regulation
Rolls Royce 102, 124–125n24

shareholdings 100, 109–113, **111–112**,
120, 125–126n30–31
skewness 16–19, *18*
small firms 3–5, 69–71, 87–88,
90n32, 92n90, **93–94**; banking
with brakes on 72–75; and the
British economy 71–72; and the
credit restrictions 75–81, **78–79**;
and hire purchase 83–87, **84**; and
the Macmillan Gap 81–83
specialisation 34, 37–40, *39–40*

staff **36**, 39–44, *39*, 49–54, 62n48,
63n65, 65–67
sub-branches **36**

Turner, John 3, 29

Union Bank of Scotland Ltd 22
Union of London & Smiths Bank **35**
University of Sussex 71

Wadsworth, J. E. 37
Wardley, Peter 3
Wednesbury 74
Western Bank 10–11
Westminster Bank **35**, 38, *42*, 49–51,
53, 73, 125n30
Whisler, Timothy 96
William Deacon's Bank 15, 22, 28
women *45*, 50, 53–54, 62n47–48

Yorkshire Penny Bank 15, 23

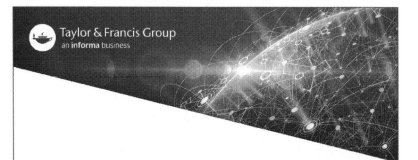